Together Again

Percy Geller

Contents

One

New Daryl Dixon fan fiction

I am dedicating this whole book to two special people

LittleMrsUzumaki and blobbish

I was simply reading one of blobbishs book when me and another reader named LittleMrsUzumaki engaged in conversation. Long story short she suggested I write a Daryl book and here I am.

Btw were best friends now.

Okay we'll ya go

--*Alyx Johns has had a brutal life. First her mother dies, then her father becomes an abusive alcoholic. She suffers beating after beating, they get worse each time.

Her life's brightens when she meets her best friend. His name is Daryl Dixon.

Alyx can't take the beatings anymore, she has to do something. She joins the military. It was the hardest decisions she's ever had to make. Escape her fathers brutality? Or leave the love of her life?

Will they make it back together again?

*_*_*

"I'm not looking for something perfect, I want something real, something between the two of us, something we both feel" I said breathlessly. We looked deep into each other's eyes, gaining the composer to speak next.

"I love you Alyx" He whispered. My heart caved in and all the hatred and anger turned immediately into love. Before I could respond his lips meet mine in a passion filled kiss

Two

5 years old

*_*_*

The full beer bottle hit the wall next to her head. He missed by inches. The content escaped the bottle in a loud crash, and little pieces of glass flew in all directions.

"You little bitch! This is all you're fault! you killed her! You're a disappointment!" The drunken man screamed at his terrified daughter. She was balled up on the corner, tears escaping her eyes. Her face was red and wet and her hands were bloody from cleaning previous smashed beer bottles.

"Go to your room and never come out! You can come out if you bring your mother back!" He yelled as he yanked her hair out of her head. She yelped as pain shout threw her skull.

"Did that hurt you little girl? Good!" he shouted and shoved her in the little closet he called her room.

Once he slammed the door she cried, and cried. She cried until she had no tears left. She didn't leave her room a long time. Minutes passed, then hours, then days. She's been curled in a ball under her bed for weeks almost. She hasn't eaten anything, drunken anything or seen anything besides the bottom of the door. She blankly stared at it, wondering when he was going to come into her room and give her what she deserved. She killed her mom. Well that's what her dad said, anyway.

-flashback-

"Mommy! Mommy please can we get ice cream!" she yelped from the back seat of their beaten down SUV.

"Honey, I don't think we can today, mummy's busy" She answered back. She texted her boss and turned the steering wheel to the left.

"But you promised!" The little girl begged.

"Alyx! Stop! We can tomorrow if you be quiet!". After realizing that she snapped on her little girl she turned her head around and looked into the girls tear filled chestnut brown eyes.

"Oh, I'm so sorry sweetie, it's just-" the mother was cut off my an 8 wheeler truck slamming into the front of the car. The little girl screamed in pain as her mothers seat flew back and slammed against her legs. The mothers neck snapped from the force of it being thrown to the side. When the little girl realized what happened she screamed her little heart out. Blood was gushing from her right leg and from her mothers cuts.

"Mommy! Help! Help me mommy!" She screamed at the top of her lungs. A crowd of people came to her side and gently lifted her out of her car seat and into the back of the ambulance.

"Wait! My mummy!" She yelled but it was too late, she was gone, and it was all her fault.

-end of flashback-

Once she built enough courage to leave her room she slid from underneath the bed. She untangled her legs and stood up. She heard multiple cracks from her stiff joints as she made her way to the door. She firmly grasped the door knob and in one swift motion opened the door.

She made her way down the long hallway and into the kitchen. When she saw that her father wasn't there she let out a sigh of relief. She wobbled to the fridge and pulled out peanut butter and jelly. She pushed her self onto the counter and stood on her tippy toes to reach the bread. Once she did she jumped of the counter with a loud bang. She cringed at the sound, scared that her father would hear. She spread the jam on the bread and then the PB. She took a huge bite out of her creation and moaned at the taste. That was the first meal she every made by herself, but it defiantly want the last.

This was her life now.

--*

Yeah first chapter, woot woot!

Watcha think?

Nope Daryl's not here yet

Neither is anyone from the walking dead for that matter but me patient my friends.

1) liking the story?

2) is it Alyxs fault her mother is dead?

3) thoughts on the characters?

Three

Chapter 2! Daryl might come in, in this chapter but you'll have to read to see...

Follow, vote, comment

*_*_*

12 years old

Alyx walked down the long dirt road. She came to a bus stop and sat on the metal bench. After a few moments of waiting for her bus a tall boy came from the tree line. He walked over to Alyx and sat beside her.

"Hey there girlie! waiting for the bus?" he asked. He was about 18years old, had dark blonde hair and bright blue eyes. He had a strong southern drawl and a crazy smirk.

Alyx didn't answer. Before her mom died, she always told her to ignore strangers. Since then she always did what she used to tell her.

"Common girlie! Answer your pal, names Merle" He lifted his hand and stuck it out to her. She nodded her head and ignored the hand.

"Girlie you better answer me before I have to kick your teeth in." He growled.

She sighed heavily and lifted her hand to interlock with his. With one shake she twisted his wrist and pushed it back.

"Ow! bitch! why'd ya do that?" He shouted.

"Alyx" she replied

"What did you say?" he confusedly asked.

"Alyx is the girl that broke your fucking wrist!" she spat. Merle laughed before taking a seat next to her. He rested his arm across her shoulder, which she gladly shook off.

"Your a feisty one. You're a little young for me though. How old are ya? 8? 9?" He asked. Alyx scoffed. She always did look younger that she was. It was probably from never getting fed or taken care of right.

"I'm 12 asshole" she replied nudging him with her elbow.

"Ooo! I got a baby brother a little older then you, why don't ya meet him?" he asked. If this boy was anything like Merle she wouldn't be interested. But having at least one friend would be nice.

"No thanks " Alyx calmly said. Merle chuckled and nodded his head.

"Okay girlie, he's a pussy anyway, why you out here all by yourself, ain't ya gotta a mom or dad?"

Alyx had to think before answering this question. The thought of her parents made tears form in her eyes but she held them back, she was good at that, she had practice. Letting out a huge breath she replied, "Don't got a mom no more, Dads at the shop" she slightly lied. The first part was true but her dad didn't leave for his job until 12, it was currently 8.

Merle pushed out his bottom lip and nodded, he understood what she really meant. Hell, he's been through the same thing.

"I get it girlie, my old mans a dick too". Hearing that from some one else, that they go through the same problems as her, Alyx slightly smiled. The conversation ended after that, and neither of them minded.

A few minutes passed and the bus pulled up to the stop. Merle helped Alyx onto the bus before climbing on afterword. She sat right behind the bus driver, Merle sat all the way in the back with his older friends.

"AYYEE!!! MERLE!!" they shouted and slapped his back. They all laughed and engaged in conversation.

Alyx wondered what it was like to have friends. She got lost in thought, thinking of all the possibilities. She was brought out of the phase when one of the older boys, Merle's friend, sat next to her. He had shaggy black hair and emerald eyes. There were small metal rings in his lip and eyebrow.

When he sat down he looked her up and down and said

"Hey there, names drake." he had a British accent and he look troublesome. He looked at her dark eyes and smiled.

"Did it hurt when you fell from heaven?" he asked. Wow cliché much? Alyx scoffed and answered how her sarcastic self would.

"No, but it did hurt when I clawed through the earths crust escaping from hell". A bunch of the other kids in the bus, burst with laughter. Alyx gave them a proud look. Drake looked at her again, but this time it wasn't with pity, it was with hatred. He leaned in really close to her, she could smell the sickly sweet scent of his cologne.

"You listen here, you may be a little girl but that won't stop me from ruining your life" he growled. He spat on her shoes and smirked. Alyx wasn't fazed by his behavior, she's dealt with much worse.

"You listen here, you may be older then me but that won't stop me from ruining your life" she growled back. Drake looked astonished, but that look was soon replaced with a look of wanted revenge.

Drake shooed the other kids away and Alyx took note in that. The bus was spilt in half, drake and Alyx in one side and the rest of the kids in the other, including Merle. Alyx hoped that if things got to out of hand, he would back her up.

Drake placed a hand on her upper thigh and squeezed. It wasn't a sexual or friendly squeeze, it was one that could make your muscles sore. She bit back her whimper and gave him a stern look. He smiled and brought his hand up her thigh, up her waist, up her sides and to her neck. Once it was at her neck he started to attempt to choke her. She acted to fast for him to comprehend. She stomped on his toe, kneed him in the groin and elbowed him in the face. He bent over in pain and screeched as she punched him off the seat and tumbling down the bus isle. A couple of the older girls started clapping and cheering things like "yeah new girl!" and "you go girl!". She smirked proudly.

Merle howled with laughter while he joined her in her seat.

"Didn't know ye had it in yah" he blurted out. Her smirk almost turned to a smile, almost.

"If someone botha's yah again I wou' tell yah to tell me but it looks like ya can handl' it." he said, looking deep into my eyes. "See yah lata' girlie" he said when the bus slowed to a halt.

Alyx was the first off the bus but the last to find her class. She finally made it to her 9th grade class when the bell rang. She was very young for her grade, she skipped a few. Her dad said she wasn't worthy, but she proved him wrong. She didn't know where to sit so she awkwardly stood in the corner. She was nervous the other kids would see her scars or bruises. She pulled down her selves and readjusted her jacket.

"Hello! you must be the new student! What's your name, sweetie?" The teacher asked. She was tall and thin. She had strawberry blonde hair and yellow glasses. The glasses made her ocean blue eyes gargantuan.

"A-Alyx.... J-Jo-Johns" she stuttered.

"Well Alyx, welcome to WestBrook High School! The only available seat is over there" She pointed to a seat in the way back corner. She slowly walked over to her seat and sat down.

In front of her was a pretty girl. She had brown hair and hazel eyes. Her skin was clear and she was wearing all baby blue. The boy next to her had light brown hair that stuck up in all directions. He was turned away from her at the moment so she couldn't see his face. He had a plaid, sleeveless shirt and dark jeans on. She wondered why he didn't have sleeves.

Probably a redneck

After hours of not paying attention it was finally time for lunch. The bell rung and all the kids swarmed out of the classroom. She was last out. Before she made it to the cafeteria a familiar face stopped her from entering the large room.

"I told you I would ruin your life" He growled. It was Drake. Alyx wasn't afraid. She didn't feel scared, she felt the adrenaline course through her veins. She's dealt with douche bags like him, what's one more? She was going to fight back, and win.

She stole a phrase she read out of a book. "If your gonna ruin it, I'm going out with a bang, not a whimper" she snarled.

(Authors note) I got that from 'double crossbow' by songbirdie

His green eyes filled with anger and disgust. He threw a punch and it hit Alyx in the jaw. It didn't faze her though, she simply turned her head to the side and cracked her neck. When she turned back to face him his features filled with surprise and mostly fear.

Good

She jumped off her right leg and used her left leg to nail him in the gut. He bent over in pain and groaned. She then used her elbow to hit him on the back and he face planted in the ground. While he was on the ground she kicked him in the side. He groaned again and reached to clutch his side.

"I told you, I would return the favor." She growled in his eyes before strutting towards the cafeteria.

When she first walked in all eyes turned to her. She avoided there stares and sat at the nearest table, it was empty, thank god. Right after she sat down the boy who sits next to her in class walked over.

"You're in my seat" he hissed.

"I don't see your name on it" Alyx hissed back. The boy sighed and sat across from her. Alyx was stubborn, so was the boy, but Alyx won.

"I don't wanna sit with you" he said with his head in his hands.

Being Alyx she replied as sarcastic and sassy as she could.

"Oh no, should I get you a blanket? Rub your feet? You wanna cookie? is that what you want?" She asked sarcastically. The boy looked into her light blue eyes and sighed again.

"Whatever" he mumbled. Alyx looked back up at him and caught his features. He had the prettiest blue eyes she's ever seen. He had squinted eyes, like he was always glaring.

"Alyx" she said sticking out her hand. The boy looked at her hand, then her face, then her hand.

"Daryl"

--*

Yeahhh, new chapter!

Look who it is! fetus daryl! whoopee!

1) do you think Daryl and Alyx will become friends?

2) what will Merle think about Daryl and Alyx's relationship?

3) what happened to Drake?

Four

Chapter 3! If your enjoying the story tell me!

I'll try and update at least once a month. Probably more.

*_*_*

16 years old

"Alyx! Come out here now!" The drunken Father raged. Alyx was hiding in her new favorite hiding spot.

Alyx did all the cooking and cleaning, she new every crook and cranny in the house. Her favorite spot was in the kitchen. Under neath the island, there were two cabinets. When you opened them they each had 3 shelves. Alyx removed the shelves and there was enough room to hide 2 people. Her father never checked here so that's where so always stayed.

"God dammit! Alyx! Get out her before you regret it!" he screamed. He was getting closer to spot. His voice echoed through the house. She heard his feet stomp and stop right in front of the cabinet. He ripped the doors open and saw her terrified face. In one swift motion, she was out of the cabinet and running down the hall.

He was faster though. He barely got a hold of her hair and pulled. She stumbled back and hit him on the chest. He grunted before dragging her to the basement door.

"I told you, you would regret it" he hissed at her before throwing her down the basement steps. She tumbled down for what felt like an eternity .

When she finally reached the bottom pain struck through her whole body. She checked her body for major injuries and found none, which should soon change.

He grabbed her hair again and ripped her shirt in half. He pulled on her arm and dragged her to the two poles. He tied her right wrist and right ankle to one wall, and her left wrist and left ankle to the other. He circled her, whipping the belt across the walls.

"Why don't you listen?" he hissed before striking her straight down the back.

"Things would be better if you were never born" he growled.

Snap

Another hit the the back. She arched her back in pain and groaned. She bit back the scream as another snap was made.

"You killed your mom" He rose his voice.

"You'll end up killing your brothers!" He screamed. Alyx hated that he always brought her twin half-brothers into this. Ethan and Grayson did nothing to him, they were only toddlers and they didn't even live with Alyx.

"You're probably end up killing me.... and that boy that uses you" He whispered in her ear.

"He doesn't use me!" She yelled and snapped her head back to hit his. He touched his forehead to feel a warm liquid pouring out. His face turned red with rage.

Snap

Snap

Snap

*_*_*

"Are the' fresh?" Daryl asked, concern in his voice. He pointed to the bright red scars sticking out of her collar. Alyx looked into his bright blue eyes as she nodded. The brightness in his eyes faded and was replaced with pure hatred.

"I swear..." he stopped himself. He couldn't swear, he couldn't stop her father from the things he did. He couldn't stop his father from the things he did.

Alyx brought Daryl to this waterfall to tell him something. She though this was the right place. Secluded, peaceful, and no one could hear his shouts.

"Daryl I have to tell you something" She started. Daryl nodded his head, he was nervous.

Is she gonna tell me she's likes me? Is she gonna tell me she's moving? Is she gonna tell me she hates me?

His mind didn't stop thinking of all the possibilities. He was so absorbed in thought he missed what she said.

"Hmm?" he hummed, telling her to repeat it.

"Well, I'm, uh, I-I" she stuttered.

"Spit it out, alyx" Daryl pushed.

"I'm leaving" She blurted out.

"Leavin'? Where ya goin'?" He asked confused. Was she leaving forever? What's happening?

"I'm joining the military" she said, looking at her feet.

"What? Why woulda do that for? Which branch?" He said raising his voice.

"The Army, and you know sure as hell why" She raised her voice to, she was starting to get angry.

Daryl's facial features where filled with anger, disappointment and mostly fear. If she left him, he would be alone. She can't leave him! Just like his brother did. Just like his mom did.

"Ya can't jus' leave! You would do that ta me? Ta yer brothers?" He shouted swinging his arms in her face. When he was angry he got physical, but he would never hurt Alyx. He clenched his fist at his sides and his breathing picked up.

"I'm sorry Daryl! I have to leave! I can't take it anymore! Ethan and Gray will be fine, they live with their mom.." She shouted back, she was done with her father, she wanted to be as far away from him as possible, even if it meant leaving Daryl and her brothers.

After realizing what she was talking about Daryl calmed down, slightly. He sighed and unclenched his fists. He walked closer to Alyx and put a hand on her shoulder.

"When yer leavin'?" he asked. He wanted to make his last moments with her memorable.

"Well, I have to be 18 to join, so a week" she calmly replied. Her birthday was in a few days, she had to wait.

Daryl looked astonished. He new she'd be leaving soon but a week?

He grunted and paced back and forth.

"Daryl talk to me" Alyx pleaded. Daryl had no more words. His actions spoke for him though. He stopped in his tracks and turned to her. He stepped towards her and put his hands on her cheeks. Before Alyx could react he forcefully connected his lips with hers. He pulled away a few moments later with tears in his eyes.

"I understand... go" he whispered. He didn't want her to see him cry so she zoomed over to his new motorcycle. He pulled his cross-bow over his head and out it on the back of the bike. Before he left he turned his head towards her.

"Stay safe, Alyx... I love you"

Alyx hasn't heard from him after that in 10 years.

--*

Whoa whoa whoa Daryl?? what are you doing? it's only chapter 3!

1) how will Daryl and Alyx reunite?

2) will Alyx survive combat?

3) what's will happen next?

Five

OoOoOoOoOoO present day chapter

Ahhhh

Here

Daryl maybe? maybe?

*_*_*

AimBreath

Shoot

One down, too many left to go.

Bang

Bang

Bang

They're still coming, they won't stop coming.

"Alyx! lets go!" Rider shouted from behind me. I finally gave up and hopped over the chain link fence. It slowed them down, but not enough.

-flashback-

"Sargent Johns! We need you in Department C, now!" General Rider yelled from down the hall. I grabbed my camo jacket and AK-47 before rushing of the camp grounds.

"Are those... people?" I asked gunning the ones who were trying to... eat everyone.

"Not anymore" Rider started. He shot two more before continuing.

"Virus broke out... Kills em' them restarts the brain stem, they are dead, but there alive... you get it?" he asked. I shot 5 more... things.

"Like it just gets them moving? but why do they eat people?" He stopped shooting once the rage dialed down.

"Do I look like a fucking scientist to you?" he sarcastically asked. I laughed and shot three more.

"Absolutely not" I muttered.

"Whatever, we gotta move, grab your shit and get in the truck, we are getting the fuck outta here" he yelled as he headed to his tent.

I ran to my bag and grabbed the whole thing except a camo tank top, military jacket, black jeans and my combat boots. I packed multiple hand guns, shot guns, automatic guns, and grenades.

I ran over to Rider and I saw that he was packing the camouflage jeep with food, water and artillery weapons.

"You pack melees?" I asked stuffing my bag in the passenger seat. He nodded his head and hopped into the drivers seat.

I took one last look at our old military base to see it infested with... walkers, hmm that's a good name.

"We need to find my brothers" I said firmly. Rider nodded and turned his attention back to the road.

-end of flashback-

"We gotta move, we ain't got time like this! we can't be held up in this building for ever! were running out of food and water" Rider informed me. I didn't listen for the rest of his rant, my mind roamed elsewhere.

First it started by asking "what would've happen if I wasn't at camp?" then I thought "what if I never joined the army. " At the back of my mind Daryl and my brothers kept wanting to join the party. Every time I thought about them my Heart shattered all over again. Daryl told me he loved me... 10 years ago...but still that was the last thing he said to me. Does he still? is he even alive? Gray and Ethan are 15 now, will I ever see them again?

"AJ! are you okay?" Rider asked. I looked at him and gave him the look.

-hey another flashback hehe-

It was the first night after training was completely over and we were going to out first battle. My bunkie (Rider) was snoring away above me.

How can he sleep at a time like this? isn't he nervous?

He jolted awake and hoped down and landed with a thud.

"Alyx? you awake? I heard you whimpering" that's true I was and I am ashamed. I haven't cried or whimpered since I was 7. it was the first night that he... he...

"I'm thinking about someone that I had to leave before I left he told me he loved me and now I don't know what to do" Daryl kept entering my mind no mater what I did.

Rider looked down at me and smiled, he then leaned close and patted my shoulder.

-end of flashback-

I have him the same look now, then I did that night. He leaned forward and have me a tight hug.

"We gotta go" he said.

I was going to reply but was cut of my gunshots. I ran up the building steps to the roof.

"Look a survivor!" I shouted and pointed the the man in the sheriffs uniform.

"We gotta get him" I started, but we were to late someone beat us too it. there was an Korean Boy running towards him and leading into an alley.

"That's the clothing store, we can go through the tunnels to get there" I suggested. He agreed and of we went

Once we were in the same building as them, we heard shouting. We ran oh to there floor and peaked in. There was the sheriff, the Korean, a blonde women, a black man, black women and a Hispanic man.

The black man was the first to spot us.

"The hell are you?" he asked. The blonde drew her gun on us but we kept ours down.

"I'm Sergeant Johns and this Is general Rider. You can call me Alyx though" I said. The sheriff looked impressed as Rider stuck out his hand.

"Hello, I'm Rick" the sheriff said. The blonde women said her name was Andrea and the black women's was Jacque, the Hispanic was Morales, the black man was Tdog and the korean was Glenn.

There was more gunshots and Morales asked something that caught my attention.

"Is that Dixon?"

"Dixon!?" I asked with excitement. They all looked at me confused but before they could talk I rushed up to the roof. I was hoping for Daryl but Merle would do.

I saw a bald man with a leather vest popping of rounds at the walkers below.

"MERLE!" I shouted. His head turned in my direction, His hard, cold, dark eyes turned light and soft when he saw my face.

"Girlie? no way!" he said as I ran to him. I wrapped my arms tightly around his neck and he patted my back.

"Daryl?" I asked. His features turned happy as he chuckled.

"Back at camp"

--*

Whoa long chapter hoot shit! I wanted to fit Merle and Alyx re-union in here so that's why it's long.

(The picture is of Rider)

1) how will Daryl react to alyx's reappearance?

2) will Merle and Alyx make it back to camp?

3) predictions?

Six

(That's Alyx)

So I've been thinking about a Daryl point of view.

Yes?

No?

Tell me what

you wanna see happen

--*

Merle was being a dick, like always. It got too out of hand.

(authors note- see what I did there?)

Anyway, he made racist and sexist comments, they were so bad that Rick intervened and handcuffed Merle to a pipe. I didn't object, he had to be controlled. But I would flip shit if he was left there. Glenn and Rick made a plan to cover them selves in guts and walk the streets. It was a stupid ass plan, but it just might work.

They were half way down the street when it started to pour. The guts were washing off. fuck.

Morales said it would last for a minute but he was wrong. The rain was horrible, it was a storm.

Rick and Glenn ran off to the fence when the walkers started to chase them. They hacked away at there heads and necks before they made it over the fence.

Once they were over Glenn got in a sports car and blasted the horn, trying to leer them away from us. Rick got into the cube van and came back to get us.

The walkers were breaking in and we had to get out of there fast. Everyone ran down the stairs, to the van.

"Tdog! Get Merle!" I yelled as I dragged Rider out of the building.

Me and Rider were at the bottom of the steps when Tdog came back, with out Merle.

Without thinking I dropped Riders arm and ran back up the steps. There is no way I'm leaving Merle.

"Rider! go with them! I'll meet you guys back at there camp!" I yelled as Rider got into the truck and I ran to Merle.

I was cut off by a swarm of walkers. I had all my weapons on me but no ammo.

"Shit" I muttered as I stabbed one. I turned my route around and ran out the back door.

The alley was empty, I ran to the nearest building and jumped in through a broken window.

Clear

I looked around for roof access and saw the bright red sign that read 'roof'. I walked towards it and broke open the door. 500 steps later I was on the roof.

I looked to the left and didn't see Merle. Looked to the right and.... there he was.

"Merle!" I shouted across the roofs. He leaned up and squinted.

"Girlie? I thought y'all left me!" he groaned tugging in the hand-cuff.

"It doesn't matter anymore, I'm coming" I yelled. I took a few steps back and sprinted. once I was at the end if the roof I leaped. my foot barely landed on the edge. I stumbled over to Merle and knelt beside him.

"Okay, my knife isn't sharp enough to cut through that chain and neither is that hack saw" I said pointing to the saw.

He looked confused before understanding what I was talking about. He groaned and got into a positions were I could get a clean cut.

"Wrap your belt around your elbow" I ordered.

"You sure you no what you're doing there, girlie?" he questioned. I sighed.

"Yes I know what I'm doing, I amputated quite a few limbs in my time at war, okay? now are we going to play 20 questions or are we going to get out of this shit hole?" I growled. He chuckled.

"Okay, go ahead" he muttered.

"This is going to hurt like a bitch, here bit on this" I said as I began taking of my camo jacket. With it off you could see my scars but he's seen them before. He nodded and put it in his mouth.

I blew out a puff if hair and placed the knife on his wrist.

Here we go

*_*_*

"Merle we have to cauterize the stump" I informed once his hand was clean off.

"Girlie...ahh! fuck! okay, comon!" he groaned. I tugged on his good arm and brought his down the steps. we made it to a small kitchen area with a working stove.

"You got a knife? can't use mine, it's got blood and dirt all over it" I said. Merle nodded and gestured towards his hip. I Pulled out the hunting knife and let the flame engulf the steel. Once the blade was red hot, I gently placed it on his stump. The blood sizzled and the skin burned as Merle let out a blood curling scream. Once i was done he let out a sigh of relief and I tucked away his knife.

"That hurt like a bitch" he mumbled.

"Don't worry, the skin will heal over the stump and it will look, well... horrible" I said with a smile. He chuckled and headed towards the open window.

"Okay, your first" he said as he gripped the chair for support. I climbed through, as he did after me.

I looked over the railing, and saw thousands and thousands of walkers below. I got dizzy and almost passed out but Merle snapped me out if it.

"Alyx" he called. That was-one of the few times he's called me by my name.

"This way" he called again. I slowly walked over to him, heights aren't my thing. Every time I looked over the balcony my stomach would so flips.

When I was in reaching distance of Merle I held onto his shoulder for dear life. He looked at me confused and then chuckle, again. For a guy with one hand he sure does laugh a lot.

"Ther's a ladder ove' ther'" he said pointing to a ladder laying down behind us. "and ther' an open winda ove' ther' " he said poring to a broken window on the building next to us. We can't use the ladder to get down to the floor, there's walkers down there.

"No..no I can't do that" I pleaded, shaking my head violently. He wants us to balance the ladder on the railing and walk across it to the open window 20 feet away.

It was the only way.

"God dammit Merle, you go first" I ordered. He chuckled, again...

I held the ladder in place while he easily strutted across. He made it look easy as fuck.

(Authors note: did you ever realize that fuck can be used as something good, bad, amazing, horrific and shit? like it's also a noun, adjective, verb, adverb, you can make a whole sentence just with fuck)

I very ungracefully climbed over the railing and onto the ladder. I grabbed hold of the ladder with both and hands and slowly crawled across. Once I was half way there the ladder started to shake. I turned to look behind me and saw that the ladder came of the rail and was swaying side to side. Merle was holding onto the other side so hard his knuckles were trying white. I had to hurry up.

"Fuck fucking fucked fuck fucking fuck" I mumbled under my Breath.

Authors note (see? it works)

One more step and I was off the ladder and inside the window.

"Fuck you Merle" I said nudging his side.

--*

Woah! there it is!

Still no Daryl... hmmm

1) Do you want a Daryl point of view?

2) what will Daryl do when he finds out Merle and Alyx got left behind?

3) will Alyx and Merle make It back?

Seven

DARYL POV RIGHT HERE RIGHT NOW IM EXCITED FOR THIS I HAVE A PLAN A REALLY CUTE PLAN OMG I CANT WAIT

HAJSBSKWNHS

YOURE WELCOME

--*

Daryl's POV

The arrow left my bow in a flash and lodged it slef into the deer. Once it felt the impact it ran off in the other direction.

"Shit" I mumbled under my breath as I followed the trail. I came to a large opening next to a small waterfall. It reminded me of the time I last saw Alyx...

I don't know how I feel about her. I did love her, I loved her like my sister. But now, I don't know if I love her in that way. What am I even saying, I'm never going to see her again, she's gone, dead. I'll never see her again. I've been wishing that I would see her again. If I do, I don't know what to do. would I hug her? Kiss her? Yell at her? I don't know if I'm angry or happy or scared. She's the reason I'm always mad. She left me and crushed me. I know why she left, but I wish there was another way. Why couldn't she come live with me? I didn't want her near my father. We were only 17 when she left, we couldn't support ourselves alone. That's why we didn't move away together. Maybe she didn't ask because she doesn't like me. She doesn't love me like I love her. I don't want to love her, I don't want to love someone who's gone.

"They never come this far up the mountain" a familiar, raspy voice softly said.

I walked further into the direction of the voice.

"They're running out of food in the mountain, that's why" a different voice said.I spotted the people towering over a deceased body. The walker was eating my dear.

When I exited the tree line, they rose there guns.

"Son of a bitch" I exclaimed, making my way towards the dead deer.

"That's my deer!" I said once again.

"Look at it, all gnawed on by this, filthy, disease-bearing,motherless, poxy bastard!" I shouted, while kicking the dead body's side.

"Calm down son, that's not helping" Dale said.

I got close to him, my blood was boiling. Not at dale, or the deer, it was always Alyx that made me angry.

"What do you no about it, old man?" I questioned.

"Why don't you take that stupid hate and go back to 'on Golden pond'?" I spat.

I sighed and started removing my bolts from the deers body.

"I've been tracking this deer fer miles, gonna drag it back to camp, cook us up som' venison, what do ya think? do ya think we can cut aroun' This chewed up part, right her'?" I asked, tracing the bit marks with a bolt.

"I would not risk that" Shane said, playing with his shotgun.

I sighed again. "that's a damn shame. I got some squirrel, dozen or so, that'll have ta do" the dismembered walker head starting snapping its jaw.

"Come on people what the hell?" I asked shooting a bolt into its head, "gotta be the brain, don't y'all no nothing?" I asked ripping the bolt out of its eye. I started back towards the camp.

"Merle!" I shouted once the RV was in view.

"Merle! get your ugly ass out here! got us some squirrel!" I shouted, looking around him. Shane stopped me from going any where else.

"Daryl, just slow up for a bit, we need to talk to you" he said.

"About what?" I asked.

"About Merle, there was a.. a problem in Atlanta."

"He dead?" I asked, my heart slightly breaking. Yes, Merle was an asshole, a racist and sexist bastard but he's my brother.

"We're not sure" Shane said.

"He either is Or he ain't!"

"No easy way to say this so ill just say it" a unfamiliar man said, breaking me and Shane's glaring contest.

"Who are you?" I asked, irritated.

"Rick grimes" the man replied.

"Rick grimes, you got so something you want to tell me?!" I shouted, greeting close to this Rick.

He let out an unsteady breath before replying. "your brother was a danger to us all, so I handcuffed him on a roof, hooked him to a piece of metal. he's still there"

I turned away from him, my eyes watering.

"Hold on, lemme process this. your saying you handcuffed my brother to a roof, and you left him there!?" I shouted, getting angrier by the second. Another unfamiliar man came from behind Rick.

"My friend, she went back for him, she hasn't returned either" he said.

"Who the hell are you?!" I yelled/asked.

"General Rider, US army." he stated.

"Well, Rider, why would your friend, go back for my bro?" I shouted. The man took a long breath, tears waiting to fall out.

"She said she knew him, was really close before all this started." He said, looking at the ground. I tried to think of any girl who would risk there life for my brother. No it can't be.

"What was this girls name?" I asked, my voice softening.

"Alyx Johns"

*_*_*

Okay so I felt this was a good ending point for this chapter.

Sorry it's so short!

1) Should the next chapter be in Daryl pov?

2) how will Daryl react to Alyx saving Merle?

3) when will they reunite?

Eight

I decided to make this part Alyxs pov and Daryls pov*-*-*

Alyxs point of view

"youre worthless! how could you think that dixon boy cares about you? you killled your mother! do you think he wants a killer?" my father screamed in rage.

snap

snap

snap

"this is what you deserve! you should be dead! why arent your screaming?!" he bent down and close to my ear. "he hates you, you need to leave before he leaves you, i dont want anyone besides me, hurting my little girl"

snap

snap

snap

"just stop! he doesnt hate me! he cares about me way more than you do!" i spit in his face. "he would never hurt me" i whispered the last part for effect.

snap

snap

snap

*_*_*

i jolted awake, and took in my surrondings. I am in a small concrete room. I am surronded by blood and sweat. I checked my body for any injuries that would have caused the pool of blood. I felt a sharp pain in my lower calf and looked to see I kicked the wall, hard. A few toes were definatly broken, the kind of break were bones stick out in crazy directions. The break looked like it went all the way up my ankle and stopped in the middle of my calf.

"fuck" I mubled as I attempted to stand up. As soon as I put the slightest amount of weight on the leg, agonizing pain shot thorugh the whole right side of my body. I managed to crawl to the nearest table in the room. With a lot of difficulty, hopped on the the table. I slolwy brought my leg up to look at the wound. I removed my boot and rolled up my bood covered jeans. I mumbled another fuck as i looked at the bumps of bones protruding from the skin.

I rembered a time in Afghaninstan where a bomb went of close by my troop. The impact caused many people to go shooting of into different directions. Rider was one of them. That was a scary moment, i thought i lost the only person i had left. He was chucked back and landed on his arm. It was the same kind of break that i have now. Thinking hard I rembered that the only way to treat it without actual medical teams was to pop the bones back in place as best as you could, then wrap it up as best as you could.

This is going to hurt like a bitch. There was a total of 3, that i could see, bone fragments sticking out. The first one was on top of my right foot. With i swift push and a blood curling scream one bone was in. Two more flick of the wrist and more then a dozen screams later my foot was in walking condition. I dug in my backpack for some new clothes and someting to clean the cuts all over me. I took out army pants, a black tanktop, black boots,and the same camo jacket as before. I changed with a struggle and used the old tanktop to wipe away dry blood on my body. I took ot the half full bottle of water i had and gently poured in over my foot. I cringed at the contact, it hurt but it was also refreshing. Riders injury was much worse then this, now i get why he screamed so much. Speaking of tough guys. wheres Merle?

"merle!" I called out, despertly wanting a reply. I limped to the only door in he room. I firmly grasped the doorknob and pushed it open. It slowly opened with a loud creak. I looked around the hallway, it was completly empty. Where am i and what happned? I felt a aching headache enter my head casuing me to fall to my knees with my head in my hands.

Daryls POV

"Alyx Johns"

No, no way, i heard him wrong.

"what did you just say?" i said so queitly i was barely audible.

"Alyx Johns., She was in my troop, Shes one of my closest freinds, we got out together." he repeated as if i were retarded. Alyx? My Alyx? it cant be possible, or maybe it can. i stared at Rider, my eyes piercing his. My heart pounding out of my chest, my mouth hanging open in shock. Everyones looking at me like i have 3 heads.

"just tell me where they are so i can go get em" i said, chocking back tears and screams.

"I'll go with you" Rider says.

"I'm going back" Rick adds in.

"Me too" glenn and tdog say in sync.

"my day just keeps getting better and better, dont it" i snap as i grab my crossbow adn head to the cube van. I hop in the back and lean over the seat to honk the horn.

I need to find her before sh leaves me...again.

Alyx's POV

The memories of the preivous events come flooding back to me

"Merle! go! I'lll lead them away! Meet me back at the apartment building!" I yell as I pop of my few rounds.

"Girlie I aint leavin you!" he yells back as he climbs up a fire escape.

"Merle, go! If i dont make it, tell daryl I missed him!" I yell back. I started climbing a different fire escape. He nods before mouthing i will and scurring up the steps into an open window. My head aches and my body throbs, but i keep fighting, keep fighting is what they teach you in the military. They say fight to the death, dont stop fghting until the enemy is demolished. Something that they dont teach you is how to control your fear. Im terrified that ill die and wont see daryl again. Ten years of fighting for my country but a lifetime of fighting for myself. The feelings overpower me. Fear, Sadness, Anger, Sorrow, Hatred. I let out a extremely loud scream and fall to my knees. Every walker in a mile raduis turns towards me and runs full speed. Fuck. I leap into the nearest window and run to down the long dark hallway. I come to a stop when i stand infrot of a metal door leading into a smalll concrete room. I fall to the floor and let the darkness take me.

daryls POV

"NO! NO!" i yell at the hand that lays on the floor in a pool of blood. Rick trys to calm me down but it just makes me angrier.

"just shut up, man! you dont get it! i lost her again" i yell in his face. He looks confused as do he rest of the guys. Rider walks towards me with realization corssing his face.

"wait, your.. NO WAY!" he starts to chuckle. "your the guy?" he asks. I have no idea what he is talking about.

"what guy?" i ask, despret to hear what he has to say.

"the guy! dude, come here" he says and gestures for me to follow him alitle ways away from everyone else.He puts his hand on my shoulder and leans in quite close. "the first couple nights of training she used to have these nightmares. I asked her what they were about and she said they were about a guy she left." he starts. She cried over me. He starts to chuckle again. "your the guy who told her that you loved her before she left?" i turn red.

"um, yah thats me" i awkawrdly choke out.

*_*_*

end of this chapter

daryls pov and alyxs pov

1) god dammit! when will they reunite?!

2) whos pov do you want next?

3) whats going to happen to Alyx?

Nine

Alyx's POV

My head pounded like a bass drum. The pain was agonizing, horrific, absolutely terrible. I will fight through the pain, I will find Daryl.

My feet managed to keep me standing as I limped out of the hallway. I came to the main entrance and found it empty. I wiped the sweat of my forehead and made my way towards the main door. With multiple try's I got the door opened. I trotted through the alley and came to an abrupt stop when a line walker jumped out at me.

I yelped in surprise and reached for my knife on my waist. When I had a clear shot, I aimed and threw the knife. It hit the walker right between the eyes. I smirked triumphantly as I went to retrieve my hunting knife. I bent over and ripped the knife from its head. When I stood to my full height I heard a whistle come from behind me.

"Damn chika, your legs look real good I'm them shorts, what are ya? Army?" A man asked looking at my butt and army pants I cut into shorts

"Shut the fuck up or my legs will be the last thing you see, and yes respect your military, dickhole" i spat. All of a sudden there was yelling coming from a different alley. I started to run toward it when the Mexican man from before stopped me.

"Hold up, chika, those my boys, why don't you come meet um?" he suggested. I nodded and walked towards the yells. I planned on getting out of here first chance I have but what if the telling is Merle? or even Daryl?

We turned a corner to see a young Hispanic boy getting beat on by a different man. The man had a crossbow on his back and was wearing a sleeveless shirt. Wait, no... no way

"Daryl!" I yelled, trying to get his attention. His head snapped up and his blue eyes completely changed. They were dark and cold, when he saw me the turned soft and they even brightened.

"Alyx-" was all he could managed to say before another Hispanic man kicked his side. I tried to attack him and scream but a bag was put over my head and my wrist were bind behind my back. I stomped on my kidnappers foot and elbowed him in the face. He let out a scream and hunched over in pain. My already disgusting, broken leg was kicked from behind which made me tumble to the ground.

A cold knife was pressed to my throat which made me stop struggling

"Daryl-" was all I spit out before I was stuffed into a mysterious car.

*_*_*

Daryl's POV

"Daryl!" I familiar, feminine voice exclaimed from In front of me. I stopped beating on this kid and looked up to be meet with those crazy chestnut eyes. The girl I thought was gone forever stood in front of me. I wanted to run to her and kiss her and yell at her for leaving me and them kiss her again, But I couldn't move. My heart dropped to the floor when a bag was thrown over her head and a leg lodged itself into my side.

"Alyx!" I managed to croak out as I was repeatedly punched and kicked. Glenn ran in from the other side of the alley. he dropped the bag of guns he was set out to get, and was then stuffed into the same car Alyx was.

"No!" I yelled as the car drove off. My blood boiled, my eyebrows were scrunched in anger. My head was throbbing and my heart felt as if someone ripped it out and lite it on fire.

"You son of a bitch!" I yelled as I attempted to kick the kid. Rick came from behind me and held be back.

"What happened?" Rider asked looking at the guns and the kid. I was to angry to answer but I manger to choke out the words 'Alyx, assholes, Glenn, drove off'. they all looked at me astonished.

"Alyx was here?" Rider asked, a ghost of a smile forming on his lips. I furiously nodded and grunted. I held myself together and told them the whole story.

"This little dickhead and his friends jumped me. They took Glenn and Alyx! They came over here and saw me, but they took um'! they fucking took her, man!" I growled. Rider looked the most shocked out of them all.

"We'll get them back, but we have to be smart about this" Rick announced. I didn't listen to him, the anger over powered me. I grabbed the little douche and dragged him into the nearest building. We tied him to a chair while Rick tried to interrogate him.

"We just need to know where our friends are" he told the boy. The boy shook his head and refused to spill. An idea popped into my head so I acted fast. I reached over into one of the bags and pulled out Merle's severed hand.

"You wanna see what happened to the last guy that pissed me off?" I growled. I threw the hand into the kids lap and smirked as he cringed and fell out of his chair. Rider slapped my back and reached for the kids throat. He held him up in the air.

"Maybe we'll start with the feet next time" he growled in the kids ear. The kid whimpered and tried to get out of Riders grip but failed. Finally the little bitch gave up his camp and led us there.

We came to a large building with two huge metal doors. They opened and a different man from before came out. Surrounding him were his little troopers, one was the same guy that took hurt Alyx. I raised my crossbow at him, if we get into a battle, he'll be the first one I shoot.

"Miguelito, how ya doing little man?" The leader asked the kid.

"Comon, G, they threatened to cut off my feet" he whimpered. G looked at Rick and then at me.

"Cops do that?" he asked.

"Not him, the redneck and the solider" he replied. G then looked at me and Rider.

"That's cruel man" G said.

"I wouldn'ta don it if ya hadn't taken out people!" Rider shot back. G looked confused, then realization crossed his face.

"People? as in plural? I got an Asian and a fine piece if ass but that ain't yours, that's mine" he exclaimed. My face turned red with anger along with Riders.

"Don't talk about her like that!" I growled, aiming my bow at his head. G started to chuckle and whistled. Two tied up figures came out from a shack on the roof. One was struggling while the other stood there calmly.

"That girls got fire, she already tried to escape 3 times" he informed. A scream was heard and I looked up expecting it to be Alyx but it was coming from the guy who was holding her. She head butted him and ripped the bag off her head. She turned around and punched the guy in the face with both her hands. He fumbled backwards and fell off the roof. She kicked the guy who was holding Glenn in the back causing him to fall off as well. She quickly untied Glenn and held his hand as they jumped off the roof and landed gracefully on a dumpster.

"Someone get that bitch under control!" G screamed to his minions, but it was to late Alyx and Glenn ran off into a different direction.

"Ha, She ain't a bitch" I said as I pushed the kid into his group. I shot the guy who hurt Alyx in the leg and we all out if there sight.

Alyx POV

Once we were far away from those nasty men I stopped Glenn and grabbed his face.

"Glenn listen to me, we have to ind the others okay? here take this" I told him as I handed him my pistol that was on my boot. I was left with my hunting knife and my bow. I really need to make more arrows.

"Can you find our way back to the roof we first met at?" I questioned. He furiously nodded his head and took my hand in his. He lead me back to the roof we first met, there was no one there. I let go of him and ran to the edge of the roof. I peered over the edge and saw what I wanted too. Daryl, Rider, Rick and Tdog were wandering the streets in search for us. I took my bow and shot the ground in front of Daryl. He looked around until he spotted me, I waved my hands trying to get his attention, in which I did. He saw me and pointed in my Direction. Minutes later they burst through the roof doors and came swarming out.

"Daryl" I mumbled before running over to him. He had his arms open waiting for me to jump into them. I wrapped my arms around his neck and lifted my legs around his waist. My leg burned but I ignored it, I savored the moment. He grunted when I launched at him before chuckling into my hair. He set me down and I looked into his Georgia blue eyes.

"Hi" He whispered.

"Hi" I whispered back

--*

Finally!

Hi I'm Alyx and I found Daryl, oh wait I'm getting captured. I get free, yay, now I run away, ha Alyx logic

1) will they get together?

2) does rider have feelings for Alyx?

3) Will Daryl lash out on her about leaving?

Ten

Daryl's POV

She here, she's actually here. Alyx, my Alyx is here, with me. All these emotions I've been feeling since she left, they took over me. I'm always angry, stubborn, grumpy and just plain mad. She was the only person I've ever connected to. Then I remembered why I felt this way. She left me, just left. Like my mom did, like Merle did. That's why I was always angry.

We had your hands interlocked and just stares into each others eyes. Then the thoughts hit me again, I could never forgive her for leaving.

I swiped my hands away from her and glared.She looked taken back, she should expect this! She just left!

I grabbed her arm and pulled her away from the group, to talk privately. Her face changes from hopeful to horrified.

"What's wrong?" she asked, as if she was, oh so innocent.

"God dammit Alyx! Was wrong? imma tell ya was wrong! Ye fuckin' left! Jus' left! Do ya no what that did to me!?" I raised my voice. She flinched back when I started to yell, but I didn't feel bad, I was to mad.

"I'm sorry okay?! you sure as hell no why I did!" she shouted back.

"I could've handled it! I coulda protected ya! Ya didn't trust me?"

"That's not it and you no it! I had to get away, can't you just accept that?" she said in a low tone before storming back to the group.

Alyx's POV

I can't believe he's still not over that. Fucking jeez Daryl, can't he just be happy I'm back?

I limped back to Rider and threw my arms around his neck. He chuckled into my shoulder before whispering into my ear.

"You are a tough son of a bitch, did ya know that?" he said. I laughed lightly.

"So I've been told"

"What happened to your leg?" he asked, when he realized I've been limping.

"It's broken, no biggie, I handled it"

When me and Rider let go of each other I caught Daryl's eye. He had a different emotion in his blue eyes. Fear? no. Anger? no. Sadness? no. It was jealousy. I smirked at the thought of Daryl being jealous, it was funny. I leaned over and hugged Rider once more before we all gathered our things and headed back to camp.

--*

Bang! Bang! Bang!

Gunshots were heard in the distance. Shock and worry filed all our faces as we hurried back to camp. The smell of decomposing flesh hit us like a snake strangling its prey. We made it into the cloud of people to find walkers everywhere. I didn't know these people but I would not let them die.

I rushed to the nearest, vulnerable person and shot all the walkers near them. It was a dark haired wen holding a crying little boy in her arms. I aimed at a walker that was to close for comfort and bang, dead. Rick rushed to me and took care of the two people, they were probably his family. I saw a young blonde haired girl cornered by two walkers. I took out my knife and threw it into one of them. the other stumbled towards her but I was to late, the walker took a huge chunk bout of her forearm. Andrea rushed over to her yelling her name and trying to stop the bleeding. I had an idea to keep her from turning.

"Andrea, Amy, we have to cut it off, it'll stop the infection from spreading" I told them. Andrea nodded furiously and Amy didn't move at all, she was probably too shocked.

I told Andrea to hold Amy down while I took off my jacket and wrapped it tightly around her arm. I picked off my knife and quickly cleaned the walker blood off it. In one swift motion her elbow and down was off and she was gushing bleeding. I told Andrea to hurry and get towels or something and she came back minutes later. Amy passed out, from the pain or shock, and Andrea was close behind. I wrapped her arm best as I could and turned to look at the rest of the camp.

There were walkers and dead bodies everywhere. Daryl was staring at me from a distance, as was Rider.

Sooner or later people mourned over there loses in there tents, except for me and Andrea. I didn't leave her side. Andrea turned to me and smiled slightly. We lost many people including Jim and Carols husband Ed, but fuck Ed, he was an assbag who abused his wife and child.

"Thank you for everything you did, for saving her" Andrea said looking down at Amy's unconscious body.

"Don't thank me until she's up and running" I said with a small smile. I patted her shoulder and turned to walk away. I felt a cool breeze blow past and it made me shiver. I went to tighten my jacket around me when I felt nothing on my shoulders. I quickly whipped around and made my way over to Andrea and Amy.

I kneeled down next to Amy and unwrapped the jacket from her arm. It was covered in blood and dirt and it was just plain nasty. I asked Andrea where I could wash it and she pointed to a big quarry near the camp. I nodded a thank you and dashed over to the water. I didn't want people to see them, my scars. They'll think less of me, they'll think of me as a kicked puppy. I don't want there pity.

I washed the jacket as fast as I could And hung it up to dry. Minutes, hours passed before it was dry enough to wear. When I climbed my way back up the hills to camp everyone was arguing. And by everyone one I mean Rick and another man named Shane. Shane was pushing towards traveling hundreds of miles to Fort Benning, a military camp, while Rick wanted to go to the CDC. Both were terrible ideas but I sides with Rick. There was no way any major military bases where still operative.

"Shane, Fort Benning is gone, no military bases are still safe. The one I was stationed at collapsed within days." I told him. He grunted and shook his head. Rider chimed in to back me up.

"Yeah, all of them are gone. Our colonel said that all military bases would be gone within the start, he was right"

Sighing, Shane rubbed his head and nodded, giving in.

"Alright now, I've known this man along time" he a started, referring to Rick, "and I trust his gut. If thinks we should go to the CDC then I'll back him up" he finished. Was he kidding? Not even a minute ago he was fighting against him and now it's all flowers and sunshine?

"What about amy? will we just put her in the RV?" I asked. Rick looked down at his feet then at Shane. Lori cleared her throat as Amy started to flinch. Andrea rushed to her side again as did I.

"Amy? Amy? can you hear me?" Andrea asked. Amy eyes opened and her lips curled into a smile.

"Hey guys" she said casually. I chuckled before sticking my hand out.

"Alyx Johns" I said as she shook my hand.

"Ah.. I know you, your my savior" she choked out. I laughed lightly and nodded my head. She looked down at her newly formed stub and scoffed.

"This is gonna be fun" she mumbled, standing up. When she rose to her full height she began to wobble. I held her good arm while Andrea steadied her by her back.

"Let's get you inside" I said as we opened the door and brought her to the back of the RV. When she was settled Andrea stayed behind to talk to her while I went to go with the rest of the group. Dale, an old pleasant man, stopped me.

"Alyx? right?" he asked. I nodded.

"Daryl flipped when Rider told him about you. Are you guys old friends?" he asked. I didn't feel the need to give him a sob story so I simply nodded again

"You are talkative aren't you?" he joked.

"Something like that" I said as I left the RV.

"Alyx!" Rick called from his car. I hurried over to him and asked what the plan was.

"Were leaving in a few minutes. Your with Rider and Daryl in the pick up" he stated. I nodded hesitantly before gathering my things and throwing them in the the bed if the truck. Daryl was already waiting in the drivers seat when I hopped into the passengers. He grunted as a hello. I grunted back to play his little game. He seemed to be annoyed that I responded the way he did but he can bite me. Moments later Rider walked over to the truck. When he saw he was stuck in the back seat his face contorted. It was funny actually so I let out a small laugh. He jumped In he back seat. He was asleep in seconds and it was quite impressive. Daryl started the truck and drove off following the trail of cars.

After hours of defining silence I opened the glove compartment.

"What ya lookin' fer, girl?" Daryl mumbled. I ignored his question and pulled out a CD of Imagine Dragons. I pushed the CD into the player and we listened to the first track that played. It was Radioactive, ironically enough. I softly sang along and tapped my foot against the dashboard. Daryl looked at me confused before brushing my feet off the dash and groaning.

"Keep ya feet off, don't ya no nothin'?"

Sighing, I took my feet down. I hummed along to the song as it played.

I raise my flags, don my clothes

It's a revolution, I suppose

We'll paint it red to fit right in

Whoa

I'm breaking in, shaping up, then checking out on the prison bus

This is it, the apocalypse

Whoa

The album ended and daryl sighed happily.

"finally, was tired of that shit" he said. I pouted and imitated his words

"finally, i was tired of that shit" i repeated. He groaned again beofre chuckling lightly. He looked down at his knuckles before stealing a glance at me. I smirked at how much of children we were.

"look, im sorry-" He was cut off by the CDC coming ito view. All the cars pulled into a parking lot and filled out of the cars. Andrea came rushing over to my side, panting heavily.

"Ita Amy, i think its infected " She said. I nedded and put a hand on her shoulder.

"maybe theyll have some disinfectant" i suggested. She nodded before running back ino the RV.

"comon guys! lets get a move on!" Shane called. I turned to the truck to wake Rider when i ran into a brick wall. Wait nevermind, it was Daryls chest. He looked down at me before smirking. Not just any smirk, the Dixon smirk. i shook the thoughts out of my head and raced oveer to the truck. iI took out my bow and hunting knife. i strapped the bow over my shoulder before pulling out a shot gun and a psitol. I tucked the oustol into my boot anf the shot gun in my hands. I went over to the truck window and baged on it like i was a walker. Rider jolted awake and pulled his gun fomr his hip. When he saw it was only me he sighed and wiped the sweat from his forehead. I laughed lightly as he crawled out the door. He mumbled a curse before grabbing his bag and weapons from the bed.

We all started towards the main doors when the walkers started to "wake up". They metal doors where shut and weren't opening.

"Rick! Its helpless!" I shouted as shane tried to rip him away from the entrance.

"No! the cameras I saw them move" he shouted, posting to the security cameras. He shouted bloody murder until the doors flew open with a loud creak, and a bright light flooded out.

*_*_*

The endings kind of boring but my phone shattered and it's hard to type without cutting my thumbs.

1)what's going to happen between daryl and alyx?

2) how do you feel about amy living?

3) is daryl jealous of Rider and Alyx's relationship ?

Eleven

So I didn't fix my phone, so the chapters will be somewhat shorter than usual..but I'm getting a new one in a few days!

Sorrrrry!! I got a cut and it started bleeding last chapter sooo, yeah

Last chapter I kept Amy alive, how do you guys feel about that?

I've been thinking about changing my username, any suggestions?

Does anyone no some really good daryl fanfics? I ran out of good ones.

Okay sorry, here's the story now

*_*_*

The light was blinding. A muscular arm wrapped around my shoulders and guided me into towards the light, along with everyone else. I recognized that arm to belong to Rider.

We all slowly made our way into the building, the light softened, and I could make out a tired looking man, with a rifle.

"why are you here? What do you want? " he called out. Rick answered, being the leader of the group.

"A chance" He answered.

"That's asking an awful alot these days" the man replied.

" I know" Rick said. All of us inched closer to the mysterioud man. Daryl was close to my side, will Rider was on the other. Me and Rider shared uneasy glances before advancing towards the man. The man backed up a few steps.

"you all admit to a blood test, thats the price of admission" He announced. Rick nodded furiosouly.

"we can do that" he exclaimed.The man lowered his rifle and walked towards us.

"you got stuff to bring in, you do it now. Once this door closes, it stays closed". Me, Glenn, Tdog, Daryl and shane ran out the door and gathered the groups belongings. Tdog slamed the doors shut behind us and the man locked them. Rick introduced as and the man did as well, His name is Edwin Jenner and he's a scientist. We made our way into the cramped elevator, I was squished in between Riders back and Daryls chest. The elevator shook and I stumbled backwards causing me to slam into a brick wall. Wait, nope it's Daryl's chest again. He looked down at me and gave me that Dixon smirk. I lightly smacked his arm and rolled my eyes, the smirk grew.

"Doctors always gon around packin heat like that?" Rider asked, to break the silence.

"There were plenty laying around, I familiarized myself' Jenner replied. Back to awkward silence.

"But you all seem harmless enough" Jenner said. He eyed Carl and a small smile grew on his lips.

"Except you, I'm going to have to keep an eye on you" he whispered to Carl. Carls cheeks flushed and he hid in his mothers side. More silence. The elevator doors opened and everyone filed out, gasping for air. Jenner led us down a long hallway and into a huge room full of computers.

"Vi, hit the lights" he announced to the empty room. The lights flashed on but no one was in sight.

"Where is everyone? the staff? the workers?" Rick asked. Jenner looked down at his feet and sighed.

"It's just me, I'm all that's left" he announced. Everyone let out small gasps as they looked around.

"What about the person you were speaking with? Vi?" Lori called out. Jenner looked at the big screen in the middle of the wall and announced

"Vi! say hello to our guest! Tell them welcome"

A rob arid female voice echoed throughout the room.

"Hello Guest, Welcome" it said.

"I'm lol that's left" Jenner repeated. Rick looked around the room, astonished.

"I'm sorry" Jenner apologized. His words made me lightheaded. I grabbed Riders arm for support as I slightly stumbled forwards. He steadied me and ask if I'm okay,Which I lie to and say yes.

Jenner begins to take our blood samples, when he comes to me, I hesitate. Zombies? eh. Spiders? eh. Serial killers? eh. Heights and Needles? Hell no. He looks at my terrified face and chuckles.

"Needles?" he asks. I shake my head furiously.

"Needles and Heights" I answer. He chuckles again and motions me to sit down. I walk over and plop down on the chair. He winks at Rider and sets the needle down.

"Hey, Alyx?" Rider calls. I turn my head in his direction, but before I can reply the needle is stuck into my forearm and I wince. Jenner pulls it out quickly and smiles to him self.

"That was rude" I joked as I stood from the chair and walked over to The group. I Sat between Carl and Daryl. Cark giggled and turned to me with a amused look on his face.

"What's up, little man?" I asked, ruffling up his hair. He whispered sown thing to Sophia before giggling again.

"We thought you weren't scared of anything!" he blurted out. I playfully glared at the two and folded my arms.

"I'm not" I said. Cark rolled his eyes and giggled again.

"Except needles and heights" he said. He giggles sown more before I lightly snakes his arm. He laughed some more before controlling himself.

"What are you scared of?" I asked the two little kids.

"Spiders and monsters" Sophia whispered. She put her finger to her lips and giggles again. Carl didn't though, he simply shrugged and looked me straight in the eye.

"Losing people" he softly said. I felt my heart break when he said that. He was so little and has to witness this horrible world. So much death, so much killing. I put my arm around his shoulders and sighed.

"Me too kiddo" I whispered kissing his head.

--*

"Children in Italy and France drink wine!" Dale said over the table. He was trying to persuade Lori to let Carl drink some wine. I honestly didn't see the issue , I mean he may never be 21 and able to drink alcohol.

"When Carl is in Italy or France he can have some then" Lori stated, putting her hand over Carl's glass. I chuckled and leaned my head on Riders shoulder. I was exhausted and all this alcohol was making me a little dizzy. Daryl grunted from the other side of me, jealous probably, but he has to grow up and accept that I left, but I'm back now.

"Come on!" Rick persuaded. Lori finally caved in and lifted her hand from the glass. Dale poured a small amount of wine into Carl's glass. Cael brought the glass to his lips and poured the liquid down his throat. Secons later he pulled the glass away and made a disgusted face. He yelled ew and said that it was nasty. I chuckled and reached across the table and ruffled his hair again.

"What don't you stick to soda pop, there bud?" I said. He smiled at me and nodded. Shane being the douche bag he is, stopped all the fun.

"So when Ya gonna tell us what happened here? all the other doctors? we came here for answers and we got one man, why?" he asked. I sighed and shook my head.

"We're celebrating shane, no need to bring this up now" Rick said. Shane scoffed and put his fork down.

"Man, this was your plan, to find all the answers" He said with a fake laugh. Jenner looked over to Shane and sighed again.

"Many just left, went to be with there families, others bolted" He firmly replied. Shane didn't look pleased.

"Every last one?" he douchely asked.

"No, many couldn't face walking out the door. there was a rash of suicides, they opted out" He said.

"But you didn't,wave, why?" Andrea asked.

"I just kept working, hoping I do some good" Jenner said. Rider rubbed his face and groaned.

"You are suck a buzzkill, man" Glenn said to Shane.

--*

Chapters long enough

Ending sucks, whoops

1) will Amy survive the amputation?

2) what's going on with the CDC?

3) is daryl still jealous?

I'm thinking of changing my username, any suggestions?

Twelve

"The housing facilities are powered down so you'll have to make do here, Theres a bed and a couch in each room. There are only 7 rooms so you'll have to double up. There's a reck room down the hall you kids might enjoy, just don't plug in the video games or anything that draws power. And go easy on the hot water" Jenner informed as he lead us to the sleeping headquarters.

"Hot water?" Glenn questioned.

"That's what the man said" Tdog said. I turned to Rider to see if he wanted to share a room but he was ready bunking with Glenn. I sighed and looked around for someone else to partner up with. They only options were Shane, Dale or Daryl, No way Shane and being with Dale would be weird so... fuck. I groaned and turned to walk to Daryl's room when I ran into another brick wall. Who was putting these here? Whoops, its daryl...again.

"You need a partner?" he asked. I sighed and noddded. He took my hand in his and lead me into the room. There was one one cot and a couch. I mumbled another fuck. I Love Daryl, he was my best friend, but he is such an asshole and I don't want to get into a relationship like that right now. I ran to the bed and leaped onto it. I bounced on my back and laughed as I sprung up and down. Daryl soon joined me and landed to my right with a loud bang. We were both laughing and rolling around while the bed creaked. On accident, I rolled over onto him. My chin was propped on his chest and my legs where as his sides. He smirked down at me pulled my legs closer to him. Part of me wanted to pull away but the other part really didn't want to.

I lifted my head up slightly and he tilted his down. Out faces were inches apart, I could feel his hot breath on my face. I got so close to him that out lips where barely touching. I smirked and closed my eyes as he did the same. I quickly hopped up of him and ran to the bathroom door. I shut the door behind me and sighed happily. He groaned and pushed himself off the bed. He stomped over to the door and banged on it twice.

"That wasn't funny!" he growled.

"It was kinda funny!' I playfully shouted back.He banged on the door again, groaning. I unlocked the door and slipped my head through to look at him. his eyes were bright and full of passion. He looked at me and smirked. I caught his lips with mine for a quick second before pulling away. I laughed evilly and slammed the door in his face.

"That's all you get for now!" I shouted as I turned the hot water on. The burning liquid hit my skin and left red marks. I didn't mind that I was being disintegrated, I enjoyed the hot water. I used shampoo and conditioner, shaved my legs, washed the sweat and grime of my body and just stood in the water thinking. A banging at the door smacked me out of my faze. I jumped out of the shower and threw a towel around me. I unlocked the door to be met with a very angry daryl.

"What's wrong baby?" I sarcastically asked. He scoffed as lightly pushed me out of the doorway. He slammed the door shut and took his own shower. I got dressed in black sweatpants and a white t-shirt, my hair in a messy bun. Daryl came strutting out of the bathroom minutes later. His hair was dripping down his face and he had a towel wrapped spring his waist, exposing his bare chest.

"Oh, stop it and put clothes on" I ordered. He shook his head and jumped onto the bed again. He landed on his back with his hands behind his head. I stared at him for a few seconds before rolling my eyes and grabbing his bag. He sat up on his elbows to look what I was doing. As soon as he could see me I chucked the bag at his head, he fell back down and rolled of the bed.

"That wasn't funny" he mumbled as I laughed.

"It was kinda funny" I joked as I slightly opened the door.

"I'm going to the Rec room" I informed as I began down the long hallway. I came to the rec room to hear loud music playing and to see some of the group dancing. Everyone was In here except Shane, Dale, Daryl and Andrea. I poured myself another glass of wine before dancing my way over to Glenn, drunkly. He was obviously wasted and stumbled around like a walker. He lost his footing at bumped into a bookshelf causing a few books to fall from it.

"You okay there buddy?" I asked as I steadied him. He nodded and laughed Before stumbling back over to Rider and Tdog. I chuckled to myself and shook my head, from his state. I remember the first time I got drunk.

It was with Daryl, of course, and we were 16. It was a week before he knew I was leaving, and it was at one of Merle's friends parties. They're were older kids pressuring me to drink it, which I finally gave in after a lot of try's. Daryl was all protective over me, he made sure no one took advantage of my drunken body, and I thank him for that to this day.

"Hey" a husky voice said from behind me as it snaked its long arms around my waist. I turned around and lightly pushed his hands of my sides causing him to frown. I poked his face with my finger and asked

"What's with the frown?"

He grunted and shook his head, his arms now completely away from me. I pouted and looked over my shoulder, to see of anyone was looking at us. Everyone left the room, surprisingly, so we were completely alone. The music was still blasting and there was empty glasses all over the room. I snaked my arms around his neck and pulled him towards me, with such force that our lips automatically connected. He wrapped his arms around my back and traced small patterns on the exposed skin. I tugged in his hair causing him to moan slightly and causing me to smirk against his lips. He slid his hands under my shirt and felt all along my back and sides, tracing some scars. My heart rate quickens when he rubbed his tongue along my bottom lip, begging for entrance, which I certainly granted. We explored ever corner or each others mouths before pulling away slightly so that we could look into each others eyes. My palms were sweaty, knees were weak and my arms were heavy. i opened my mouth to speak but no words came out.

"Finally" he mumbled against my neck, where his face was now buried. I laughed softly, his body vibrated against mine, as he did also. Second later Sophia and Carl burst through the door laughing. They came to an abrupt stop when they saw me and Daryl wrapped around each other. They turned red and giggled. Sophia whispered something to Carl and he burst out laughing. I quickly took my arms from around Daryl and brought them to Carl and Sophia. I tickled them both until they begged me to stop.

"What was so funny?" I playfully growled. They looked at each other before giggling some more.

"You were kissing Daryl!" Sophia shouted. I looked over shoulder at him to see him smirking with his arms crossed. Ugh, that fucking man will be the death of me. His muscles bulged out of the short sleeve shirt he was wearing, his legs crossed, and he's head slightly tilted upwards. His blue eyes pierced mine and my breath hitched. I turned back to face Sophia and Carl to see that Sophia was laughing into her hands and Carl was wiggling his eyebrows. I sighed and ruffled up both there hairs.

"Ugh, kids" I mumbled as I stood to my full height and turned down the music slightly.

"Well, I'm going back to the room, is anyone coming to watch you guys?" I asked Carl and Sophia.

"Mom" Sophia said and gestured towards the now open door with an amused carol standing in the doorway. I nodded and waved to her, then made my way out of the room and towards me and Daryl's.

Halfway down the hall I felt a presence behind me. I turned expecting to see Daryl but I was meet face to face with a very angry Shane.

"Um, hey Shane" I nervously greeted. His eyes were filled with anger and lust. I silently planned an escape if things got to out of control. He came closer to me causing me to take a few steps back but stopping when my back hit a solid wall. He put his hands on either sides of my face, trapping me in his grasp.

"You look fine tonight darlin'" he whispered into my ear. I hid my fear, guys like Shane eat that stuff up. I ignored his comment as I attempted to free from his grasp.

"Where you going, darlin' we just getting started" he drunkly slurred. I saw movement coming from my right, before I could process what was happening Shane was in the floor with Daryl beating his face in.

"Daryl!" I shouted as I tugged in his arm, getting him to stop. After Shane got in a few punches, as well as Daryl, they both calmed there selves. Rick and Rider were holding Shane back while I was containing Daryl. Both my hands were in his chest and I was whispering soothing things to him.

"It's okay, calm down, he didn't hurt me" I said. His heart rate was back to normal, finally. I lead him away from everyone else and dragged him into our room. I sat him down in the bed and straddled him. I took a clean rag and dipped it in ice old water. I dabbed his wounds on his face, he would flinch back and swat my hand away when I tired. I tried talking to him but he just ignored me and continued staring into space.

"Daryl, it's over now" I told him, trying to look him in the eyes but he avoided my gaze. I took his chin in my thumb and pointer finger and tilted his head up to meet my eyes. He looked me straight in the eye and slightly nodded. I leaned in ever so slightly and connected out lips, again.

*_*_*

Whoa! daryl and Alyx action?

1) ship name?

2) Shane's an asshole, agree or disagree?

3) I can't come up with another questions so uh, save the rainforest?

Thirteen

Over 550 reads?

God damn

--*

Alyx's POV

"Mommy! Wake up!" I little voice calls from down the hall. I jolt out of my bed and ungracefully land on my back. The small body of a 6 year old girl jumps on my stomach.

"Hi sweetie, what's wrong?" I ask concerned. The dark haired girl looks down at me with big blue eyes, just like her daddy.

"Daddy made pancakes, and he burnt em'" she said, nonstop giggling.

"Did he now?" I ask while standing up with her on my hip. She nodded and smiles a big toothy grin. I chuckle at her cuteness and walk down the hallway to the kitchen. Here I find a handsome, partial clothed man cooking breakfast. I set my daughter on the couch and wrap my arms around his torso, kissing his shoulder. He looked down at me a nervously smiles.

"Uh, I tried to make ya some breakfast" he nervously mumbles. I smile and take the spatula from his shaky hands.

"It's fine, baby, they look great" I lie. Our daughter comes running from the living room laughing like crazy.

"No de don't! Dere black, momma!" she laughs. Daryl playfully glares at her and darts towards her. He lifts her into the air and tickles her until she can't breath.

--*

I woke up to the soothing sound of Daryl's soft snoring. I stare at him while I try to comprehend that dream. Did I like Daryl enough to start a family with him? I don't even no where we stand, and I'm thinking about a child, and marriage?! ugh, this dream.

I turned over on to my side to me met with his slightly ajar mouth and relaxed facial muscles. He looks so calm when he's sleeping. His jaw isn't clenched and his eyebrows aren't furrowed. He looks almost peaceful.

"What'cha looking at there, babe?" His husky voice echoed through out the room, his eyes still wielded shut.

"Babe?" I asked with a smirk. His eyes fluttered open and he smirked as well.

"Don't go changin' the subject" he jokes while reaching his arm over and flinging it around my waist. His arm lays lazily on my waist while his fingers okay with the hem of my t-shirt. I chuckle softly and scoot towards him, giving him a quick peck on the lips. He attempts to lean into the kiss for more action but I back away. He pouts and his eyes fill with lust and passion.

My heart rate speeds up when he take my wrists in his one hand and pins them above my head. He supports his weight with his free arm as he hovers over my body. He dips his head down for a few seconds of sweet bliss. I wiggle on of my hands free and push on his chest lightly. He pouts again as I gain control and straddle his hips. I feel him grow hard against me as I rock back and forth. I reconnect our lips to keep my moan quiet. We pour so much emotion into that kiss. It's hard to explain when you kiss someone like this. Someone you love. It's not something you can put into words, it's just a crazy feeling.

There's a knock at the door and we both groan. I stand up, off of him, and open the door.

"You coming to breakfast?" Rider asks as he leans against the door frame. I sigh and nod. I turn to look back at Daryl and find that he's in the same position I left him except now his arm is shielding his eyes. Rider nods and darts to the main room, looking for, apparently he's new best buddies, Glenn and Amy.

"Let's go, babe" I put emphasis on the babe to tease his word choice from before. I start down the hall way when a strong hand gets a firm grip on my wrist. I turn, not sure who to expect.

"Wait" the husky southern drawl says to me. I let out a sigh of relief when it's just Daryl. A look of nervousness flash in his mouth before he speaks again.

"I'm sorry" he says, looking at the ground. I gave him a confused look and gently freed my wrist from his grasp.

"I'mma apologize, when ya left, I couldn't hold ma self together. Yer were right ta leave an' I don blame ya" he said. I nodded my head and reached my palm up to rest on his cheek. He leaned into my touch before kissing my hand softly. I smiled, an actual smile, he did too. I love the effect I have on him. I've only seen him smile about 5 times in the 20 years I've known him. I leaned in and brushed our lips together for a quick second before pulling away just as fast. I smirked at his surprised face, he playfully glared.

"Yer such a tease" he growled. I laughed and leaned on for another kiss. We were centimeters apart when I pulled away and darted down the hall. I heard him groan and chase after me.

He caught up to me seconds later and grabbed me by the waist. I let out a small squeal, that I am completely ashamed of. He chuckled and carried me over his shoulder towards the main room. When the doors came into view he dropped me and held both my hands. I was going to tease him again but this felt right, I wanted to kiss him. He inched closer to my face, at the last second he moved to the right and planted a sloppy kiss in my neck. I gasped in surprise before pushing him off and slapping his shoulder.

He smirked at me and quickly opened the doors and targeted his prey (bacon).

"Hey guys" Glenn said while wiggling his eyebrows. I flicked his forehead and reaches over for the eggs. I made my plate and sat in between Carl and Rider. Daryl stood over my the table and leaned on a desk.

"Are you hungover?" Carl asked Rick. I smiled to myself and reached over to ruffle his hair.

"Mom said you'd be" Carl said. Lori smirked as well as Rick.

"Mom is right" Rick answered.

"Mom has that annoying habit" Lori said with a sly smirk.

Tdog came into the room with a plate full of scrambled eggs.

"Eggs. powdered, but I do them good" he called. Glenn groaned in pain and Jacque went over to rub his shoulders.

"Protein is good for the hangover" T said as he poured a bunch of eggs onto Glenn's plate.

"Where's all this come from?" Rick asked, gesturing towards a bottle of medicine.

"Jenner" Lori answered.

"Can you help me please?" Rick asked.

"He thought we could use it, some of us at least" Lori said as she opened the bottle of pills. Rick thanked her and downed a bunch.

"Don't ever, ever, ever, let me drink again" Glenn moaned.

"I'll think about that" Amy pitched in. She's doing okay, at least I think. I stood up and walked over to her.

"How you doing?" I asked.

"Better, thanks to you" she smirked

"Well, I did my best, and you ruined my jacket" I added. She chuckled and dove into her food. I patted her back and went back over to my seat. I was about to sit down when Shane walked in and took my seat. I glared at him and leaned into a desk by Daryl.

"Officer asshole take yer seat?" he teased.

"Oh ha ha" I coldly answered back. Shane had three claw marks on his neck.

"What the hell happens to you?" I asked. Shane looked over to me then to Rick then stared at Lori for a while.

"Must'a done it in ma sleep" he lied, obviously.

"Never seen you do that before" Rick said. Shane held his state on Lori.

"Me neither" he said. I nudged Daryl and gave him a spectacle look. he shrugged and continued eating his bacon.

"We didn't come her for the eggs" Andrea suddenly blurted out. Jenner looked at her and sighed before leading us to the late computer screen.

*_*_*

Another sucky ending, ew.

I really want to get to the prison but we still have to farm to go so ugh.

1) is the CDC safe?

2) what's going on within Dalyx?

3) does anyone else ship Rider and Amy?

Fourteen

Molly, I know you're reading this

Doing a time jump right now because the CDC episode requires a lot of word for word lines and ain't nobody got time for dat

Also I've been trying to respond to your comments but it always errors, just know that I love all of you for commenting!

*_*_*

BOOM

The last 'safe haven' we had, destroyed, exploded, obliterated, engulfed in fire. The CDC exploded into pieces of destroyed ruble and flames. Jenner told us about the walker infection. It shuts down the brain, the human part, it's gone forever. The brain stem restarts, gets the bodies around and moving, just enough to attack live people. The CDC ran on fossil fuel, which they ran out of... The CDC would go through 'decontamination' when it ran out of fuel, and that's just what happened. Jenner stayed, as well as Jacque, they're gone now...

Dead. They wanted to burst into flames, a millisecond, Jenner said, no pain. He'd rather quickly die than fight on and stay alive to end this thing. But not me, I've been to hell and back but I won't stop trying to get to heaven.

"Yer okay?" Daryl asked as he lifted himself off of me, lying on the truck floor. He'd just protected my body from the heat of the explosion, but we were still dripping with sweat. Rider hopped in the RV with Glenn and Amy. He definitely has a thing for Amy, I made a mental note to tease him about that later. But now wasn't the time for games.

"Yeah, You?" I replied to him. he just shrugged so I looked into his fear filled blue eyes and kissed his cheek quickly. He turned the truck on and speed down the road after the rest of the group. I pulled my legs to my chest and rested my forehead on my knees. I sighed deeply before looming out the window at the scenery.

"What are we going to do now?" I blurted out of the blue. I turned my head to look at him, he was biting his thumb finger nail, a bad habit. He shrugged and kept his attention on the road ahead of us.

"You look like your sucking your thumb when you do that" I informed, easing an eyebrow. He scoffed and continued doing it. I shook my head and rested it back on my knees. Dar cleared his throat to get my attention, I looked at him and he was patting his lap with his hand. I sighed and laid across the front seats, my head in his lap. He brushed a piece of hair behind me ear and lured me into a deep sleep.

Daryl's POV

She looked so peaceful when she slept. Her eyes weren't wide and full of fear, her jaw wasn't ready to bite you, her eyebrows weren't scrunched together in anger. She looked relaxed, happy almost...al most. A single honk knocked me from my gaze and I looked to the road. The cars were pulled over and they were discussing something. I slowed to a halt and lifted Alyx's head of my lap, setting it down gently on the seat.

"Was wrong?" I called out. Rider walked over to me, arms crossed.

"Radiator houses busted... again. Where's Alyx?" he asked.

"Again? God dammit. And Alyx's asle-"I began

"Right here, fellas!" Alyx interrupted, sitting up from the truck seat.

"Couldn't sleep any longer, and I heard Daryl being a little bitch" She mumbled the last part to Rider, as she walked towards us. A grin grew on his face but was soon erased when I glared at him. He looked scared and backed away towards his girlfriend, or soon to be at least. (Amy)

"RV's stopped?" She asked. We all nodded in sync, Alyx sighed deeply and put her hair up in a messy bun.

"Could I take a look?" She asked dale. When everyone gave her a shocked look she turned to me.

"Redneck taught me a thing or two, plus the only thing to read at my place was car magazines." She mumbled as she grabbed a flathead screwdriver and dived into the engine.

"Besides, you shouldn't be that surprised"

I smirked when Rider nudged me with his shoulder. He was alright by me, he saved my girl...more then once.

"Okay, Everyone else let's scavenge want we can from these cars" Shane said, gesturing towards the bundle of empty cars on this highway.

" this is a graveyard, I'm not sure how I feel about this" Lori admitted. I lookedv at her with disgust, everything's a fucking graveyard these days. Rick looked at her pleadingly, and she squeezed carls shoulder then nodded hesitantly.

Dale and Alyx talked about how she learned about cars, I went my own way. I came to a stop when I heard a hushed shout. It came from a unknown voice but I listened to it. I looked around, frantically trying to find the owner of that soft, quite voice. I finally saw a young, blonde, girl hiding under a car.

"Look ahead!" she softly called. She had a bow and arrow next to her, and was signally me to look forward? When I did, me heart dropped ... Walkers ... dozens of them.

Alyx POV

I twisted the screwdriver and wrapped some more duct tape around the hose.

"Alyx, get up here now" Dale called from on stop of the RV. I was about to ask why but a hand was pushed against my mouth. I turned to see that it belonged to Rick. He gestured towards the road ahead, I realized why we needed to hide. Walkers.

I quickly scrambled on top the RV and dropped face down. The moans and groans continued to grow louder and louder before they were right in front of me.

An earsplitting scream caught me off guard and I tumbled off the RV. I landed softly on an ironically placed truck hood with a loud thud. I searched for the source of the scream when I saw Sophia being chased into the woods by two walkers. I ignored the pain in my whole body as I sprinted after her, Rick close behind.

"Sophia?" I softly called to the empty forest. She peeked from behind a tree and ran into my arms. Rick ran from the tree line close behind me. He sighed in relief when he saw Sophia safely in my arms.

"Take her off that way" he said pointing in the direction of the highway. "I'll lead the walkers off this way" he ordered. I nodded and picked Sophia up bridal style, and ran away from the walkers that Rick was killing.

Minutes later, I still couldn't find my way through the twist and turns of the mucked up forest trail.

I heard a branch snap and quickly pulled out my gun and set Sophia down behind me. She whimpered into my shirt as I slowly searched for the causer of the sound. A young girl, maybe 13 or 14, plopped down from a pretty high branch in a tree.

"Whoa, whoa! I ain't gonna hurt you" She pleaded, holding her hands up in surrender. She had wavy, dirty blonde hair and a bow and Arrow strapped around her shoulder. I lowered my gun and took a step closer to her.

"Are you alone?" I asked. Se hesitated before shaking her head furiously.

"I got lost from my sister, we were on a run. My pop owns a farm, you could come to it with me" She offered.

"What's your name?" I asked as Sophia started to look up at the girl.

"Riley Greene, You?" she asked.

"Alyx Johns. This is Sophia" I answered sticking out my hand for her to shake. She firmly shook it and told me the direction of her farm.

"I need to get back to the highway before deciding if we could go with you, I just can't find my way back" I confessed.

"I'm not sure where it is, I was there recently, ran off though, the people we're scary." she said, shaking her head.

Our conversation came to an end when we heard the growls of hungry walkers.

"Let's go!" Riley yelled, yanking my arm and ripping me away from the herd of walkers. I tripped on a branch and stumbled forward, dropping Sophia in the process. She yelped in pain and ran off into a different direction. The last thing I remembered before the light faded was Riley chasing after Sophia, leaving me there to die.

--*

(That picture is of Riley)

Back to the authors note. Molly, stop now, This is embarrassing, don't speak to anyone about this... I'm trusting you.

To everyone else who is not Molly, I hope you enjoyed this chapter and keep reading to find out what happens next!

1) Will Alyx survive?

2) how do you feel about the new character, Riley Grenne?

3) Predictions?

Also, Riley is played my Sabrina Carpenter from Girl meets world. She is awesome and I want her to be in The Walking Dead TV show really bad..

Fifteen

Over 1k reads?!?!?!

Are you fucking kidding? I'm having a party and all of you are invited. *throws confetti*

*_*_*

Daryl's POV

The walker lays unmoving on top of me as another did to Tdog. I still had the little girl under the car in sight and I wasn't planning on changing that. Dozens of limping walkers stumbled there way down the highway, snarling and searching for there next meal. It seemed as if the whole world reeked of death. After all the walkers had past our group I walked over to where the girl was hiding.

"Stop!" she called out from behind the car. I stopped in my tracks and turned to her.

"I ain't gonna hurt ya" I told her, holding up my hands in surrender. She rose her bow higher and aimed it in between my eyes.

"I lost my sister, you seen her?" she asked, taking a few steps back from me. I shook my head causing her to let out an irritated sigh. She slightly lowered her bow, it was aimed at my chest.

"I'm going to leave and your not going to follow me. Okay?" she ordered. I hesitantly nodded, then I thought what Alyx would say.

Don't let her go, she's a little girl who needs your help

"Wait!" I called out, getting her attention before she ran off.

"Why won't ya stay? Gotta group ye might like" I mentioned. She sighed before running a hand through her hair.

"I'm with my family, I'm fine. Just back off" She threatened as she began to take steps off into the forest. I gave up and lowered my hands. I turned around and grabbed my crossbow when I heard a blood-curdling scream come from near by.

I spun on my heels and sprinted towards the scream. I saw a glimpse of dark brown hair chase after a little girl.

Sophia

Alyx

God dammit...

Alyx POV

The darkness slowly faded away and was replaced with a blinding light. The softness beneath me was the first indication that my surroundings had changed. I couldn't move or speak, but I could see and hear. My eyes fluttered open and I saw the same girl from before sitting in a chair across from me. I was laying down on a bed, unable to fidget even the slightest bit. My joints aches and the sensation of numbness coursed through my body. I was stiff from inactivity and inevitably to move.

Her eyes widen in shock when she saw me come too. She stood up from the chair and ran over to the doorway. My throat burned as mumbled words escapade my dry lips.

"Daddy!" she exclaimed. "Shes waken!". Moments later an old man and a middle aged woman came rushing into the room, carrying medical supplies.

"Hello Miss Johns. I'm Hershel. Can you hear me?" he said, waving his hand infront of my face. The movement made my head pound even harder than it already was. I squeezed my eyes shut. I nodded as best as I could while Hershel sighed and the woman adjusted the IV in my forearm.

"Wha-at ha-appen-end?" I managed to croak out. The middle aged women looked at me with sad, pity filled eyes.

"Riley was on a run with my other daughter, Maggie. She got separated on her and ran into you. Do you remember what I'm talking about?" he calmly replied. I nodded again causing a sharp pain to shoot through the back of my head.

"You were carrying a little girl, when you fell you hit your head very hard. The walkers that were following you, they trampled you and bruised some of your internal organs." he informed. Wait... Why didn't they attack me? More important, Where's Sophia?

"The little girl, where is she?" I almost shouted. Hershel looked at me sympathetically before whispering down thing into the middle aged woman's ear. The woman rushed out of the room and came back minutes later with Sophia in her arms.

"Oh my god, sophia" I said under my breath as she climbed onto the bed and scurried over to me. "Are you okay?" I asked her. She mumbled inaudible words before shoving her face into my side and crying softly.

"She is just scared, a minor case of shock. She has to major physical damage though" Hershel informed me. I nodded and mouthed the words thank you, in which he nodded back.

"How long have I been out?" I asked, hoping for an answer like 30 minutes.

"Almost a day" Hershel said. I gasped and shook my head. A day? That long? What was Daryl thinking? Rider? Oh my god, what about Carol?

"We have to get back to our group, she needs to be with her mother" I pleaded. Hershel kept shaking his head, along with the middle aged woman, I really need to know her name.

"You are in no condition to be hopping around the woods. You have to rest for at least a day or two" Hershel said. I sighed in defeat and crossed my arms over my chest, clearly unhappy with the situation.

Maggie brought me and Sophia lunch and we introduced our selves. I've learned that the woman's name is Patricia and the big man in the living rooms name is Otis.

"So what did you do before all this?" Maggie asked me.

"I was in the Army for about 10 years" I answered. Maggie's eyes widen in shock. She then smirked and patted my shoulder.

"Impressive, trooper" She joked. I chuckled softly and looked down at my lap, I wasn't in the mood for talking.

"Any family?" she asked. The cold air wiped around me forcing the air out of my lungs. I chocked back a sob, thinking about Daryl and my father.

"I have two close friends back in the group but that's it." I said. Maggie looked at me with sad yet curious eyes.

"What about your parents?" The air tightened and it became even harder to breathe.

"My mom died when I was little and my dad, haven't seen him since I joined the military" I told her. She instantly regretted what she had said, you could see it in her facial features. She put a comforting hand in my shoulder but I shrugged it off. I decided to change the subject.

"So enough about me, Tell me about your family" I said.

"Riley and Beth are my half sisters. Their mom died to the walkers, mine to cancer a while back"

"I'm so sorry"

"Don't be, you no what it's like, don't treat me like a kicked puppy."

"I know the feeling"

"Riley gets so-" She was cut off my a single, yet very loud, gunshot. Sophia jumped from next to me and wrapped her arms around my torso.

"Don't worry, It's just Otis hunting" Maggie reassured us. It didn't work though, I felt a lump at the pit of my stomach. I nodded an okay, but I couldn't shake the feeling that something bad has happened.

Moment later some one burst through the front door, causing it to slam on the way back. There was shouting and loud footsteps soundings from the whole house.

"Sophia stay with Riley, I'm gonna see what's happening" I told Sophia. She agreed and huddled in the corner next to Riley. Me and Maggie made our ways out of the room and into the one with everyone else. There was a man sitting in a chair with his head in his hands. I walked over to him and tapped his shoulder. His head spin around and his dark, sad eyes lite up.

"Shane?"

"Alyx?"

He stood up and we embraced in a a hug. We weren't the best of friends but he was still from my group.

"What happened? why are you here?" I asked him, searching for a sign in the room. His face dropped and he stuttered his sentences.

"C-Carl... He got shot" He managed to croak out. I immediately dropped Shane's hands and ran into the next room to find carl laying unconscious on the bed with a very tiresome Rick sitting next to him.

"Rick!" I announced and engulfed him in a hug. He hugged back, but not as tight. He looked pale, very pale. He had blood smeared all over his shirt and face. The thought of such a young, innocent boy being shot made my heart sink. I counselor imagine having my only child almost be killed right I front of my eyes. I hugged Rick even tighter, he needs my comfort.

"How's everyone else?" I asked Shane once I left Rick to mourn over his injured son.

"Were all fine last time we seen um' Me, Rider, Rick and Carl split from tha group lookin' for ya and Sophia."

"Where's Rider?" I asked.

"I think he's out front" I patted his shoulder and gave it a light squeeze before making my way out the door towards Rider.

He was propped up against the railing, watching the sunset in the distance. I snuck up behind me and shook his shoulders. He shrieked and fell backwards, landing hard on a bush beneath him. I almost got a nosebleed trying to contain my laughter. He looked like he was going to punch someone until he saw it was me. His face lite up and we embraced for a few moments. After pulling away I looked deep into his blue eyes and kisses his cheek.

"I can't fucking take you Alyx" He said as we shared another long hug.

*_*_*

I know it sucks butthole but I needed to give you guys something! Molly and Julia haven't shut up, especially Julia...

1) How will Daryl and Alux reunite?

2) Will Daryl be glad she's alive or be mad that she left?

3) CAN YOU BELIVE THE WALKING DEAD WILL BE BACK IN 5 DAYS???

Sixteen

SO THE PREMIER WAS ABSOLUTELY AMAZING!!

AGREE?

DISAGREE?

--*

Daryls POV

The single gunshot echoed throughout the forest. Lori and Carol jumped and intertwined fingers.

"Was that a Gunshot?" Amy asked. I nodded along with Glenn and Andrea.

"Why one? why one gunshot?" Lori stuttered. Her face was full of terror. I get why, but Alyx is still missing, there's no time to worry about a gunshot.

"Maybe they took down a walker" I suggested, nobody believed, me not even myself.

"Don't patronize me, you know none of them would waste a bullet on one walker" Lori growled. I sighed and looked down at the ground, I just want to get back to looking for Alyx and Sophia. Carol was about to speak up when a bloodcurdling scream was heard from near by.

"Andrea!" Amy yelled and chased after her screaming sister. The sound of horse shoes clacking caused our heads to turn and stare at the women on the horse. She knocked the walker on top of Andrea over the head and started blurting out the words that were to muffled for me to hear clearly.

"Lori? Lori Grimes?" She questioned. Lori stumbled over to her answering her question.

"You have to come with me, Carl's been shot! Come on, Rick needs you." She said, taping the horses side with the heel of her boot. We all stared in shock as Lori climbed on to the horse.

"Ye can't get on tha' horse!" I called out, but it was too late, the women informed us in where they were headed before galloping off in the other direction. We all looked at each other for confirmation before sprinting in the direction of our camp.

"Shot? What do you mean shot?" Dale asked us when we got back to the RV.

"I don't know Dale. Some chick just road out on a horse and took Lori" Glenn said.

"And you let her?" Dale angrily asked me.

"Crawl outta ma asshole man, Rick sent'er. She new Ricks name an' Carls" I said, walking to my bike.

"We have to reconnect the group. Someone needs to go to that farm" Dale ordered.

"We can't leave yet, Sophia's still out there" Carol said, barley audible.

"If Sophia came back and we weren't here, that would be awful" Andrea spoke up.

"I'll stay with the RV for the night" Amy said, putting her arm on her sisters shoulder.

"If the RV is staying so am I, but I think you should go to the farm with Tdog and Glenn. See if they have any antibiotics for your arm and Tdogs cut. Its going from bad to worse, it needs to be treated" Dale said. Amy nodded obediently and started towards the car. When Dale said antibiotics I remembered Merle's stash of drugs.

"Why didn't y'all say nothin'. Got Merle's stash."I advanced towards my bike and pulled out his bag of crystal, X, and various other drugs. I dug through the bag before pulling out a bottle of Ibuprofen. I threw it to Dale along with a bottle of some kick-ass pain killers.

"That ain't generic shit neither, that's first class" I informed as Tdog popped a few into his mouth.

"Merle got the clap on occasion" I said and shrugged. A ghost of a smirk formed in my lips when Glenn nearly gagged.

"So Me, Tdog and Amy? Why do I have to be the one?" Glenn asked, irritated

"You need to get them to that farm, Glenn. T has a serious blood infection, he could die!" Dale reasoned. Glenn finally sighed in defeat and slumped over to the car with T and Amy.

"We can head ther' in tha' mornin'. Give us enough time to leave some supplies, rig up a big sign." I said, referring to Sophia's situation. Carol walked over to me and rested her hand in my shoulder.

"Thank you" She whispered. I grunted and pulled away from her.

Hours past and the sun had set and the moon has risen. I was crammed in the RV with a bunch of other people and couldn't sleep. I groaned and popped up from my spot on the floor and made my way to my crossbow. I slung it over my back and hopped out the RV.

"Gonna go search fer the girls" I informed Dale, who was keeping watch on the RV.

"You sure that's a good idea?" He asked

"Better then siting aroun' here" I mumbled as I slid over the roof of a car blocking my path. Moments later Andrea appeared at me side.

"I'm coming too" She said, nodding. I shirt he's and we began our search for my girl and the little girl.

ALYX'S POV

The chirping of the crickets and the hooting of owls were the only sound coming from the dark fields. I sat with my knees to my chest on the porch swing.

Shane and Otis went on a run for medical supplies for carl a while ago, and still haven't returned. I was getting worried, what if they weren't back in time?

It was late, almost everyone was sleeping but I was waiting. I don't really know what I was waiting for, but it hasn't satisfied me yet. I thought for a while , I let my mind wander. I was thinking about Daryl, The group, My father, My mother, the apocalypse, everything really. You know when you have a simply thought, but it continues to grow into endless possibilities. That's what happening to me.

I wonder what Daryl is doing

Probably wonder where the fuck you are

I want to find him

But you can't

Why not?

Because you're in pain, you're a coward

I'm not a coward

Then why aren't you looking for him?

Because Hershel won't let me leave

Yeah, that's the reason

It's is!

When have you ever listened to someone else's orders? You have never obeyed anybody! That's who you are Alyx! Now get off your ass and go find him! You love him!

No, I don't love him

Yea you do

No

Yes

No

Yes

The sound of an engine cut off my internal argument. I think I might be losing my sanity. Coming up the dirt path was a familiar car. The car became bigger and bigger until it was parked in front of the house. Glenn came out of the driver seat, Amy the passenger and

Tdog the back. They slowly walked up to the porch, not noticing me siting here.

"Do we knock?" Glenn asked.

"Of course" I called out. They spun in my direction and we ready to pull out there weapons.

"Go dammit! Alyx?" Amy nervously asked. I came out of the darkness and ran into their arms. We had a awkward group hug and separated quickly.

"How? What? But... Sophia?" Glenn attempted to form a sentence, all while stuttering pretty badly. I let out a small chuckle and gestured toward the house.

"They saved us. Sophia's okay, shes in there. Where's everyone else?" I answered, and then asked.

"They stayed back so wait to see if you would return. We came to fix T's arm and Amy's, um uh, stub I guess" Glenn said, rubbing his neck nervously when he said the last part. Amy smiled at his nervousness and patted his shoulder.

"Well, they do have so antibiotics for you guys" I said pointing to Tdog and Amy. I guided them into the house where they got treated and Glenn went of to try and flirt with Maggie. I repeat, He tried, and failed epically, It was comical actually. I decided to attempt to get some sleep.

I said goodnight to Rick, Lori, Maggie, and the rest of the bunch. I slept in the room I woke up in. Sophia was curled up in a ball on the other side of the bed softly crying. I could hear her but I didn't want her to know that. I'm not very good at comforting people. I tested my head on to the pillow and let the darkness over take me and lure me into a restless, light sleep.

*_*_*

I need some feedback from you guys!

1) how will DARYL react when he finds Alyx and the farm?

2) Are they finally safe?

3) again, I can't come up with another question so... Recommend me some questions I guess...um yeah

Seventeen

Alyx's POV

I was woken by birds chirping and the sun shining through the slightly ajar window. For a fraction of a second, I forgot about the walkers and the apocalypse. For that fraction of that second, the world seemed to be, if not more, peaceful then it was before it went to shit.

I lifted my head from the pillow and rubbed my eyes with my hands balled in fist. I yet out a loud yawn and turned to my side to see that Sophia was nowhere in sight.

I panicked.

I jolted out of bed and sprinted towards the doorway. My foot got caught on the leg of a dresser and I tumbled out the door and down the hall. I landed on my butt in the middle of the hall with my back facing the stairs. I didn't see the steps since they were behind me, so I laid back with my hands covering my face. Being me, my head hit the first step and I tumbled down the steps. When I reached the bottom my whole body was on fire. There were aching pain circulating through my entire body.

"Fuck" I mumbled as I adjusted my limbs into a normal sitting position.

"No cussin' in the house!" Hershel yelled from the other room. I sarcastically chuckled and attempted to stand up. My legs wobbled and my head swayed, causing my vision to be blurred. Maggie came running down the hall with her arms outstretched, ready to steady me if I needed it. I, of course needed it, but denied her help. I stepped forward with my right leg but came crashing down to the floor. Everything started to fade and I, once again, was overpowered by the darkness.

--*

Daryl's POV

We arrived at the old farm house where Carl, Rick, Rider and Shane were the day after. I forced my body to cooperate and drag my feet to the place where we will be camping out. I didn't really care about anyone else, I only wanted to find those two missing girls. They were all that mattered to me now, finding them is all I need to do. I need to, if its the last thing i do. I promised myself I would keep Alyx safe and I broke that promise. I failed her. I failed the whole group. I just want to keep her safe. Whenever I'm with her a get a numb sensation throughout my body and my mouth goes dry. Maybe I love her. I've never loved anyone, let alone a woman. The hell am I talking about, I don't. Even if I did, this "relationship" would be one sided. How could she think of me like that? All I am is a uneducated redneck. These feelings that I have for her are unexplainable. I don't understand them. Physical pain I understand, but this emotional crap? Hell no. Damn her for making me feel this way! I'll just push them a side, ignore them. That's all. That's it. I have no room for that kind of relationship. I can't get to close to her, because if she leaves, I can't be heartbroken. But I want to be with her, I want to feel her soft skin against mine and her sweet lips and to see her smile that is more beautiful than the stars. I really have no idea what I'm going to do.

--*

Alyx POV

I woke to a dark sky and the sound of glass clattering against glass. I was getting tired of waking up with no remembrance of what had happened. I moaned and rested my hands in my head as I sat up. The quiet clacking sounded like giant footsteps pounding down a metal hallway. I groaned again and massaged my temples. The pounding dialed down and I gathered enough strength to stand up. I stood to my full height and everything swayed. I lost my footing and came crashing down onto the bed. I groaned again and stood up once more, accomplishing this time. I made my way to the door and opened it.

I walked down the narrow hall way and when I arrived at the stairway I sighed heavily. I carefully made my way down the steps into walked into the dinning room. What I found made me speechless.

The group, the whole group, was sitting at the table having a casual conversation. I cleared my throat and all their heads spun in my direction. Everyone went dead silent.

"Alyx!" Carl and Sophia squealed as they ran up to me and threw their arms around my waist. I patted their heads and smiled. I bent down to eye level with them.

"Hey kiddo. You looked like you've healed." I said to carl, holding his hands. He nodded excitedly and smiled real big. I stood to me full height and patted his shoulder. The only person that wasn't in here was Daryl. I must have looked worried because Lori chuckled and shook her head reassuringly.

"Don't worry, hun. He just wanted to be by himself is all." She said as she stood up. One by one, everyone greeted me and gave me a hug. When everyone was done I took a roll of bread and headed outside to find Daryl. I took a step onto the porch and overlooked the scenery. Our tents were set up around a tall tree in the front of the house, a barn was standing a few hundred yards back and a long dirt path lead up to the house. I squinted as saw that on top of a hill to the the right was a small fire. It was Daryl's private camp. My legs automatically started to carry me to him. I quickened my pace. My lungs burned and my legs ached but I ran on.

When I was close enough I saw his built figure sitting on a log carving some arrows. I stopped in my tracks.

"Daryl?" I said, sounding hopeful, taking a few more steps towards him. He looked up at me and smirked. His smirk soon faded and anger crossed his face.

"The hell, woman?" he shouted, standing up and tossing his arrow to the side.

"Wha' the hell are ye' doin' here?" He yelled, getting closer to my face.

"They found me and Sophia and brought us here." I calmly answered. I'm not quite sure what is going on here, but I'm going to just go with it.

"Yer all nice and cleaned up here but ye' don' come lookin' fer the rest of us?!" he practically screamed. I was still attempting to keep my calm.

"Daryl, I was injured and unconscious! I had no choice." I said, getting angrier by the second.

How dare he, how dare he, finally find me and yell at me for not looking for him. I was not able to leave, I was unconscious for days!

"I was out here every single day looking fer ye! I thought ye were dead, but yer here havin' a tea party with yer new friends?" He said, pointing in my face.

"I tried to find the group! I really fucking did, Daryl! I got knocked out! Twice for fucks sake!" I yelled, my blood was beginning to boil. This was a new level of anger I was experiencing.

A single raindrop fell from the sky, it hit the bridge of my nose. It would soon start to pour. I ignored it and continued to file out my case.

"Ye seem okay to me! Yer tellin' me, tha' ye got hit over the head and couldnt come serchin' fer us?" he growled.

"Yes! Hershel wouldn't let me leave!" I hissed, taking a step closer to him. We were inches apart, I could feel his breath hitting my face.

"Bullshit" he said in a low tone. I stared at him for what seemed like an eternity.

"I missed ye" he mumbled, resting his hand on my hip.

"I missed you too." I answered, placing one of my hands on his cheek.

"Really?" he asked, leaning in a little closer.

"You have no idea." I said before I crashed my lips into his for a few seconds of sweet bliss. By now, I wasn't feeling angry I was feeling jubilant. The soft rain drizzle was replaced with powerful downpour.

It was like a romantic movie scene, expect in those there are no flesh eating monsters...

--*

Have I ever told you guys that I suck at writing endings?

1) For TWD do you ship Caryl or Bethyl?

2) Is Dalyx finally going to be, like, all lovey and stuff?

3) do you know what a sausage staff is?

Eighteen

What did you think of the Dalyx reunion?

I'm kinda unsure about it, your thoughts?

Okay guys, the fucking newest episodes (four walls and a roof and slabtown) were so good I love it.

ALL I ASKED FOR WAS A COOL ZOMBIE SHOW NOT A HEART BREAKING THRILLER ROMANCE HORROR LIFE RUINER

*_*_*

Alyx's POV (dream/flashback)

"Common Alyx!" 15 year old Daryl Dixon yelled from the edge of the dock. I took a breathe before pulling my sweatshirt over my head and running to him. He was in a pair of old shorts while I wore a tank top and shorts.

"Ready?" he asked besides taking my hand in his and sighing heavily. I could barely make out his features in the moonlight.

"1...2...3!" he yelled and jumped into the lake, dragging me with him.

The water was freezing.

"You asshole!" I joked and splashed him. He choked on some water while I attempted to swim back to shore.

"No your not!" he yelled, laughing as he swam over to me. He gripped my leg and pulled me towards him. I hit his chest and we both went crashing underwater. Since it was so dark out, I couldn't see the light from the sun hitting the surface. I couldn't tell which direction was up... I was drowning.

"Daryl!" I screamed, but it only came out mumbled. I swallowed the salty water on accident and took a descend towards the bottom of the lake.

I couldn't see, breath, hear, or talk. I was helpless.

And then, everything changed. I magically found out how to make my way to the top. This is only a dream...Only a dream... dream...

I took in a breathe and to my surprise I didn't take in water, I took in pure air. All of a sudden the water disappeared and I was back on the beach.

I was lying down next to young Daryl and he was fiddling with some seashells. I tapped his shoulder and he spun around.

He looked confused. His cheeks were raw and red, from crying... What was he crying about?

I waved my hands in his face but he continued to stare right through me.

"Daryl?" I practically yelled. He stood up and ran to the dock and sat down with his feet in the water. I could hears his quiet sobbing as he gripped something in his hand.

I stared at him intentionally as he opened up his palm. There lied a picture of us when we were about 12. We were sitting in a tree with our legs dangling. He was holding a very small sharpened stick and I had a baseball bat. We were probably hiding from our dads, we were looking out for each other. He flipped it over and on the back it read in our very sloppy handwriting 'Daryl and Alyx, protecting each other since they met'.

Daryl wiped his nose and read the note out loud. His voice cracked on my name. He let out a muffled sob before folding the picture up and bringing it to his lips. He kissed it with his eyes closed.

"I'm sorry I couldn't protect you... it's actually my fault your dead." he said, with his eyes still closed.

It all made sense now... I had drowned in that lake and he took the blame.

It's just a dream...just a dream...dream

The scene changed.

I was sitting on a stump in the middle of the forest. I looked around and then I heard two small voices. I walked in the direction of the voices and saw a boy and girl playing tag in a small opening. The boy, Daryl, was it and chasing the girl, Me. He finally caught up to 12 year old me and tapped her shoulder. She spun around and pointed in his face.

"You cheated!" She yelled, sending a death glare into his little blue eyes.

"Nuh uh!" he shouted.

"Yeah!"

"Ye don' no notin'!"

"What don't I know?"

"How t'play this prissy game!"

"You don't know how to play!"

"Yeah I do!"

"No!"

"Yes!"

"No!"

"Yes!"

The scene changed again. The young versions of me and daryl were gone and replaced with the present day versions. They were fighting off walkers, when a swarm overpowered Daryl and brought him to his knees. He screamed in agonizing pain as the flesh was ripped from his bones.

She brought my gun to his head and pulled the trigger, ending his misery. As i watched the scene unfold my heart shattered, but the other me just let it all happen. After she has eliminated all of the threats she brought the gun to her head and pulled the trigger, ending her life.

I jolted awake from that confusing dream. It wasn't all a dream, Me and Daryl did used to go to a lake by our houses and we did used to play games in the forest. The fight about tag even actually happened.

I know it was all fake but it felt so real. I hopped up to my feet and scrambled out of my tent. I shielded my eyes from the bright sun as I stumbled towards the house. I gracefully hopped over the railing of the porch and walked through the doorway.

"Hey guys" I greeted Glenn, Rider, Amy and Maggie. I smirked and wiggled my eyebrows at them causing them to turn red. Maggie took Glenn's hand and led him out the house and towards his tent. They're probably going to do the bangity bang if you know what I mean.

I walked into the kitchen and was greeted with with the soothing smell of cooking eggs. Patricia served me a plate of bacon and eggs with an orange juice. I thanked her and inhaled my food.

Once finished, I thanked her once more and went off to find something to do. I saw Carl and Sophia playing by a big tree. I skipped over to them and greeted them.

"Hey guys!" I said, waving my hand around. They looked up at me, then at each other and then they laughed.

"What?" I asked.

"Can you help us?" Sophia asked. I nodded and took a step closer to them. Carl pointed up and I craned my neck to look at what he was pointing to. I saw a little red kite stuck in the branches about 20 feet in the air.

"You want me to get that?" I asked. I am not going up there, that is way to high!

"Yes" the two children said in sync.

"We spent a few chapters on my fear of heights remember?"

"What? just get over it!" Carl playfully barked. I threw my hands up in surrender and took a step closer to the tree. I grabbed to the branch in line with my chin and hoisted my legs around it. I finished the pullover and swung my right leg over so I was straddling the branch. I bent both my legs and stood up on the branch, misplacing my footing and wobbling towards the trunk.

Once steady, I hoisted my self onto a higher branch. This continued until I was about 10 feet off the ground. This was high enough.

"I can't go any higher guys!" I called down to Carl and Sophia.

"Yes you can!!" They yelled. I groaned and continued my journey upwards. I looked down and instantly regretted it.

It seemed like 1000 feet... It seemed like an endless pit. I breathed in through my nose and out through my mouth.

"You got this" I mumbled under my breath as I reaches out and grabbed the stupid kite. Whem it's was in my grasp I hurried down the stupid tree and to the stupid kids. I dropped down from about 4 feet and threw the dumb kite at them.

"Here" I growled and messes up their hair. I heard them giggle as I walked towards my tent. I peeked over my shoulder to see Daryl giving the kids high fives. It all made sense now. I angrily marched over to the three delinquents.

"You little shit! You out the God damn kite there!" I yelled at Daryl, lightly hitting his shoulder. He smirked and the kids ran off into the house. I attempted to hit daryl again. He grabbed me wrist and looked into my eyes deeply.

"Nuh uh" he mumbled before pulling me into a passionate kiss. I smiled into it and got lost in the sweet frenzy.

*_*_*

Just a filler I know it was short and bad

These are some questions for the new episodes so if you haven't seen them do not read!

1) Who do you think was behind Daryl is 4 walls and a roof?

2) will BETH and Carol make it out alive?

3) I have school and don't wanna go to sleep... Ew

Nineteen

Alyx POV

I decided to take a walk along the perimeter of Hershel's land. I was going to think, check for walkers, maybe catch a squirrel, but I mostly wanted to just be alone. After the recent events between me and Daryl, I just needed to be by myself. I need to figure out the feelings I have for him.

I heard a twig snap from behind me and my hand instantly flung to my gun. I pulled it out and held it in front of me.

Another twigged snapped from a different direction and I spun towards it.

"Whoa, Whoa, Whoa there. I ain't here to hurt no one. Me and my boys, we just checkin' out the area." I deep voice said from the darkness.

"All of you come out!" I ordered. 5 Men and a teenage boy came trudging out, all armed.

"I'm Dave" The same man said. "Thats Tony" he said pointing to the heaviest man. "There's John, Nicky, Jay" he said gesturing towards the other 3 men. "And Randall" he said to the teenager.

I need to get them away from the farm.

"Leave" I ordered. Dave threw his hands up in fake surrender while the others chuckled.

"Why? Ye gotta camp or somethin'?" Tony asked. I directed my gun toward him.

"No" I lied.

"Then why we gotta leave?" Nicky asked.

"You don't. If you're here for food, I got it all and if you're here for a camp, it's all infested with walkers" I lied again. Dave nodded and puffed out his cheeks.

"Well, guess we gotta go then boys, lets get a move on" He said, turning his back and starting off in the direction they came.

It happened so fast...Too fast.

The butt of Jays gun slammed into my back, causing me to fall to the ground. Randall brought his foot down on my neck, suffocating me. Dave pushed him off and looked me deep in the eyes.

"You shouldn't have lied" He growled before punching me in the face, sending me out cold.

Daryl's POV

"Ye seen Alyx?" I called out to Dale. He looked down at me from the top of the RV and sighed.

"She said she was doing a perimeter walk, she left a few hours ago. She should've been back already." He said. I nodded and hurried to my tent to gather some things. I grabbed my Crossbow, Knife, backpack and arrows and hopped on my motorcycle. I started the engine and ride over to Dale.

"Imma go look fer her." I told him. He nodded and I zoomed off into the direction she went.

Something was wrong, I could feel it in the tip of my heart.

As I drove faster and farther i became more worried. Where was she? A revolting feeling rose from the pit of my stomach to the back of my throat.

Something was definitely wrong

Alyx POV

days later

My eyes flickered open and the hard surface underneath me uncomfortably stiffened my muscles. I lifted my head off the ground and felt the pounding begin. I was way too sick of this shit.

I groan escaped my lips as I attempted to stand to my full height. I felt wobbly and uncoordinated. I tried to reach my hand up to my forehead to find that my wrist were taped together behind my back. I sat back down and pulled my arms under my body and around my legs so they were in front of me. I lifted my arms above my head and forcefully brought them down, breaking the tape.

I smiled triumphantly as I ripped the rest of the tape of my arms.

Now that that is out of the way I looked at my surroundings. I was in a small, dark, wooden, room. It was almost a basement or a cabin. There were metal bars covering the only window and multiple heavy locks holding the only door shut. I hobbled over to the window and reached up to wiggly the bars, they were not even loose.

I heard a loud clicking noise and the door burst open. Tony came trudging in with more tape and a pillow case.

"Come on girl, Dave wants ye'." he growled, forcefully gripping my hair and yanking me towards him. He held me against his chest and kept a firm grasp on my hair.

"After he's done with ye, I wanna turn." He whispered into my ear. His breath smelt like onions and greasy pig. He had a cheesy like substance stained on his shirt and face. Looking at him made me want to gag.

He bound my wrist and threw the bag over my head. He must not be very smart because I could clearly see through it. He lead me down a long hallway, the same structure as the room I was in. He finally stopped when he arrived at a staircase. He pushed me up it and out the door at the top.

The sun light blinded me for a second before I was able to adjust to the brightness. Tony dragged me to a large blue tent and ripped of the pillow case.

"Get in" He growled, pushing me into the opened flap.

Dave sat on a stool at a small table. He pointed to a heap of blankets, were I took a seat. He tapped his fingers against the wood and hummed a soft tune.

"I never got your name." He said casually, like He wasn't a kidnapper.

I scoffed and crossed my arms.

"Ooh, a stubborn one...Tony's favorite, I like ones who play nicely." my eyes free wide when i picked up on what he was hinting at.

"If you don't tell me your name, I'll have Tony come in her and beat and rape your sorry ass." He said, easing his voice. I slammed my mouth shut, I was not caving in. And I was not afraid of some fat, greasy, idiot.

"Ugh, fine. I wasn't going to do that anyway. You seemed like you can take care of your self. Got any experience?" he asked.

"U.S Army." I firmly stated, leaning back slightly.

"Oh! Isn't that nice...Why'd you join?" He asked.

"That ain't none of your business!" I growled.

"Family problem?" He suggested. He must've say the hint of sadness in my eyes because his lite up.

"I'm close! Daddy issues?" he suggested again. I'm sure that I didn't change my physical appearance at all but he could read me.

"That's it!" he shouted, hitting his hands down in the table.

"Stand up." he ordered.

"No" I replied.

"STAND UP!" he said more forcefully. I rolled my eyes and stood. He scanned at my body with a look of determination in his eyes.

"Take your shirt off." He ordered. I shook my head but he pulled out a gun. I sighed and ripped of my t-shirt, never breaking eye contact.

"Turn around." he said while waving his hand Ina circular motion. I spun so my back was facing him. He gasped and then stood up. He walked towards me and gently traced a scar.

"Your dad did this to you?" he asked, not a hike of concern in his voice. I didn't answer, instead I felt a burning sensation coming from my back. It was all to familiar.

"I think I'm going to add a few new ones." he growled as he brought the whip down again.

--*

Eh...Fucking Dave God dammit

1) how will Alyx get out of this?

2) what's happening back at the farm?

3) How will Daryl feel when he finds out about what Dave is doing?

Twenty

3k reads?!?

200 votes?!?!

Yeahhh!!!!!

Another party, everyone's invited!

Daryls POV

It's been days since Alyx went missing, Sophia went missing as well. We've been looking for both of them nonstop. Glenn found walkers in the barn, Shane flipped and busted it open. Sophia was inside, but she was a walker. That hit us all really hard, especially Carl, Riley and Carol. An innocent little girl, ripped from her life and turned into a mindless monster. Rick had to shoot her...It was so bad. Carol wouldn't stop crying, she wouldn't come to the funeral. Hershel's wife was in the barn too. When he saw all of the things he called 'people' get killed, he got really depressed. He left the house and went to the bar in town. Rick and Glenn went after him. Lori went out looking for them when they didn't return. Dumb Bitch got in a car accident, with no other cars on the road! Shane brought her back and turns out she's pregnant with Shane's baby. I wonder if Rick knows. Glenn and Rick came back with another idiot as well. His name is Randall and I have to interrogate him tomorrow. That'll be fun. Ill let out all my anger and sadness onto his stupid little face.

I need to look for Alyx some more. I have this aching feeling in my heart that something went terribly wrong and I can't shake it off. She was taken, I know that for sure.

I was currently sitting high up in a tree, like she used to. Rider and I haven't stopped looking for her, but the group wouldn't let us go at night. They're scared we'll go missing too, get taken by the same guys who took Alyx.

Fuck it

I jumped down from the tree and ran to my tent. I pulled out my weapons and backpack and secured them onto my bike. I revved the engine and started down the dirt path leading away from the house. I rode down the road untill i made it to the highway. I hopped off my bike and set off on foot. About half an hour later i made it to the spot where Alyx was supoosedly taken. I looked around for clues, for anyhting. There was a set of footprints. They were small and boot shaped. They were Alyx's. I follwed her tracks untill i found some more. There were 5 other sets, one smaller then the rest. There was scuff marks throughout this spot. I follwed them, the lead me to a tree with blood splattered all over it.

oh no

Is it her's? Is it her captures? Did they kill her?

The thought of that happening...it broke me down. I collapsed on the floor in a sobbing heap. My face began to be stained with tears. I didnt care, no one was here to see me in my weakest state.

I felt a hand touch my shoulder and i jerked away from it. I look up to be met with thoses beautiful cheastnut eyes.

"Alyx?" i croaked out. She nodded her head and lifted her hand of my shoulder. I jumped to my feet and reached out to hug her. My arms flew through the empty air. She disaperred, she was a figure of my imagination. I groaned and kicked the tree with blood on it. My foot hurt but I didn't care. I am going to find her. No matter what.

Alyx's POV

The beatings are getting worse each time. Each snap the whip makes brings back the haunting memories of my past.

Of my Father

I shook the thought out of my head and thought about more important things.

I need an escape plan

I look around the small room to findabsolutely no way of getting out of here. I could try breaking the bars in the window but they looked too strong. I couldn't break down the door, it was too thick and stiff.

Think

What would Daryl do?

What would Rider do? Or Rick?

I unbuckled my belt and pulled it through the loops. I wrapped it around my hand so the metal buckle was pointing out wards. I tapped it with my finger, it wasn't to sharp, but sharp enough to cut through human flesh If I use enough force. I scurried to the corner farthest from the door and waiting until someone came to beat me again.

Each time they would try and get me to tell them where the group was but I will not betray them like that. I won't put the group in danger. These people would attack them, kill all the men, and rape the women and children. There is no way in hell I am putting Sophia, Carl, Riley, Beth, Maggie, all of them, through that.

I heard a locks on the door click and it flew open. Jay walked in with a bag and a rope. I was going to go through another interrogation. Another beating.

"Come on, honey. Time to get ye ass whipped." He growled, stepping closer to me. I tightened my grip on my belt weapon and stood to my full height. I nodded my head and started to walk in the direction of the door.

"Wait..." I said, trying to throw off Jay.

"What?" The disgusting man grumbled. I whipped around and wrapped a hand around his neck. I pushed him against the wall and stabbed the sharpened belt into his throat. He gargled before all the blood came rushing out and poured onto the floor. I kicked his side and spit on him before mumbling a 'fuck you'. I took his gun he had in his pocket and zoomed out of that hell hole. I stopped in the hallway and tried to find my way out. I went into the nearest room to find it to be an old supply closet with wooden floors and cement walls.

Think

I got down on my knees and stuck the belt buckle in between the cracks of the wooden panels. The panel came out with a pop and I picked it up and moved it out of the way. I repeated this with several other panels until there was a wide enough gap. I dived into it and crawled around underneath this building. I saw light coming from a direction and scurried towards it. There was a window that led to an open lake. I used the butt of Jays pistol to break the window and crawl out, only to hit the water below with a loud splash. I held my breath as I swam as far away from my captures as I could. I came up for air and looked behind me to see that the building was about 50 feet away. I swam farther and farther until the lake came to an end. I crawled out of the cold water and ran aways as fast as I could. I was finally out of there.

Finally free

*_*_*

Hey, she's out!

1) will Alyx make it back to the farm?

2) Will Daryl find her?

3) How will Alyx react when she finds out Sophia is dead?

Twenty-one

WARNING IF YOU DID NOT SEE THE MID-SEASON FINALE OF TWD SKIP OVER THIS SECTION

*_*_*

Okay so about the finale. I was a blubbering mess. Beth's death is the only death that has impacted me this much... I loved her and she's just gone... SCOTT GIMPLE is a wazz Bag who killed her off to shock the audience. They literally spent the whole season so far trying to save Beth and Her characters development, but then nope! Lets just shoot her in the fucking face! ARGH! it makes me so mad. Daryl's heart wrenching cry and Maggie's face or dear lord Maggie's face made me want to crawl into a pit and light myself on fire.

ATTENTION IF YOU SKIPPED OVER THAT PART YOU CAN START READING HERE vvvvvv

Onto a lighter note I want everyone to go on YouTube and search up 'You're a wizard Harry'. That video is my life. Okay next chapter now!

*_*_*

Daryl's POV

"I swear! I don't know nothin'!" Randall screeched as I punched him another time.

"Bullshit!" I snarled, kicking his side.

"They w-were bad g-g-uys! I didn't do any-anything like them! I swear! We were out scavenging this one time...Came across this girl. She was real tough, real cute..." He said, looking at the floor. Was this girl he's talking about Alyx? I need to know.

"What did you do to her?" I whispered. He shook his head violently, begging me not to hurt him.

"What did you do to her?!" I yelled very loudly.

"I didn't touch her! I swear I didn't! She said she was by herself. W-we didn't want to hurt her, I swear, but she wouldn't cooperate, the guys they took her, man. I didn't do nothing though! Dude I swear!!" He begged for his life. This was Alyx he was talking about. It was his group that took her.

"Where the fuck is she?" I yelled, picking him up and slamming him against the wall. "Tell me, asshole!"

He started shaking and he squeezed his eyes shut.

"Okay! Okay, Man! Fine! My buddy, Dave... The guy your man killed, he beat her pretty bad... He whipped her, he was screaming at her about her daddy or some bull crap like that. But I swear, man, I didn't do nothing to her!"

That was it

That pushed me over the line

How dare he

How fucking dare he!

(Time jump, the next part takes place in between the farm and prison)

Alyx's POV

Minutes

Hours

Days

Weeks

I have been scavenging and attempting to find my way back to the group. I found the farm, only to be met with the barns debris and dead walkers everywhere. I camped out in a small house on the side of the road for a day or two. Just long enough to gather supplies and weapons. I really hope someone grabbed my shit before they left the farm. I need to get back to the group.

Back to Daryl

Back to Rider

My two favorite men in the world. All this time away from them has made me realize how much i appreciate them. How much I love them. Yeah, it's love, I know that now. I just hope they feel the same towards me. I love Rider like he's my brother. I Love Daryl in a different way...In a significant other way.

Stop thinking about that now though. You need to find them first. Stop thinking and Act.

I heard a twig snap from behind me and I instantly spun around. I was met face to face with a snarling walker. I reached into my back pocket and pulled out a pistol. I aimed it at the walkers head and pulled the trigger, ending the deceased corpse movement.

Daryl's POV

BANG

A gunshot rang throughout the woods.

"Do you think that was Alyx?" Carl asked while opening a can of dog food. Rick walked over to him and snatched the fan from him before throwing it into the fireplace. Rider looked at me then at Carl then at Rick.

"I don't know, Carl. It could've been." He said, gathering the feathers that I pulled off of some dead owl. Carl grinned and started to sharpen his knife when I heard the groans of walkers coming from outside.

"We got company." I grumpily grunted. Immediately, everyone began packing their shit and heading outside.

We got into our cars and traveled a few miles down the road before we came to a stop.

"While everyone washes their panties, lets go hunting." I said to Rick. He nodded his head as we began our descend into the forest to look for food.

Alyx's POV

I dragged me legs down the long, straight road when I saw a few figures and cars sitting a mile down. So I took off into a sprint in that direction. Moments later I was met face to face with a very happy, grown-up Carl.

"CARL!" I yelled as I brought him into a hug. I felt my shirt moisten as his tears of happiness seeped into the fabric. When he unlatched himself from me i crouched down to his eye level.

"Hey, Bud! How you been?" I asked, patting his shoulder. His smile soon faded and it was replaced with a heart-wrenching frown.

"Alyx... So much happens when you were gone..." He said, looking at the ground. I became very worried.

"What happened, kid?" I asked eager to find out.

"Sophia, Amy, Shane and Dale died at the farm. Andrea got lost when it was over run." He started off with. When I heard the news my eyes began to tear and I brought him in for another hug.

That hit me like a ton of bricks. All those people, i gel them so close to me... And they're just gone. I didn't even get to go to the funerals!

Carl pulled back and wiped his face."My dad found some guy named Randall...Shane killed him later though." He mumbled.

Randall

My blood ran cold. The same Randall that helped capture me. The same Randall who helped Dave whip me. The same Randall that didn't do anything to stop it.

"Anything else I need to know, bud?" I asked, my voice cracking. He nodded his head and a ghost of a smile formed on his lips. His happiness gave me happiness.

"My moms pregnant..."

"That's great, kiddo! You're gonna be a big brother!" I said while bringing him in for a bother hug. He pulled back and flicked the top of his sherif hat.

"Big brother Carl, sound pretty cool, right?" He giggled. I nodded my head and my smile widened.

"I'd say that sounds very cool." I encouraged. Our laughter was cut short when I heard yelling and the sound of heavy foot steps coming from behind Carl. I looked over his shoulder to see a very familiar figure running in our direction.

Rider

I broke out into a sprint towards him, my legs burning with every step. We lunged at each other and I was engulfed in a passionate hug.

"Alyx...Alyx! You're alive! Oh sweet damn! You're alive!" he said, picking me up and swinging me around.

"Yeah, I think so." I joked when he put me down. There was a smile plastered on his face and it looked like it wasn't coming off anytime soon. He looked different than when i last saw him. His facial hair had grown out, he's skin is a lot dirtier, his hair longer, clothes ripped and mix matched. Not to be weird or anything but he looked hotter.

I was so glad to see him. There is still one more person I'm looking for though.

"Where's Daryl?" I asked, eagerly. He thought for a second before pointing behind him. Seconds later a muscular man was escaping from the trees and heading our way.

--*

I want everyone to go and search up "You're a wizard Harry" on YouTube. If you can recite a line, I will dedicate the next chapter to you.

1) Thoughts on this chapter?

2) How do you feel about Dale, Sophia, Amy, Shane's deaths?

3) How will Daryl react to swing Alyx and her injuries?

Twenty-Two

This chapter is dedicated to oheyitsamy and jd_tybs

This amazing new cover is made by FabulousFireHydrant, <3

Daryl's POV

After finding the Prison, Rick and I went back to tell the others.

When we broke from the trees I saw a new figure talking to Carl and Rider. I nudged Rick and pointed in their direction. He lifted his gun and I lifted my crossbow as we made our way over to them. That person could be a threat, we need to eliminate the threat.

The tall, brunette girl looked at me and her legs immediately started to run in my direction. I lifted my crossbow higher, aiming it at her head. Once she got closer I noticed her copper eyes, plump lips and high cheekbones. I noticed the army jacket on her shoulders and the black jeans nicely hugging her long legs. My breath hitched in my throat and my heart was beating so fast it could've popped out of my chest.

Alyx

I dropped my crossbow and it hit the floor with a loud clank. I sprinted as fast as my legs could carry me until I was a few feet away from her. I scooped her into my arms and hugged her so tight my arms were sore.

"Alyx... I-I can't believe you're here.." I managed to mumbled into her long dark hair. She looked up at me with her beautiful eyes and enhaled deeply.

"i should've done this along time ago" I said before forcefully connecting her perfect lips with my dry ones. Our mouths moved together in sync until we separated, gasping for air. I stared into her eyes and she stared right back when a deep chuckle sounded, followed by a group of others.

We turned around to see the rest of group with goofy smiles planted on their faces. Alyx gave me a quick kiss on the cheek before dashing off to reunite with the rest of the group. She walked over to Rick first, throwing her arms around his neck and embracing him tightly. They shared a few words before she made her way over to Lori, Riley and Beth.

She turned to Maggie and Glenn to see that they had impatient looks on their faces. Glenn was tapping his foot and Maggie was gripping his hand tightly. Alyx gave Beth another quick hug before skipping over to the duo and jumping into their arms for a group hug. I didnt know she got that close with them. Im glad she did though, she needs some people to depend on.

They had a short conversation and she finally let go of the two and made her way over to Tdog, Hershel and Carol. She gave Tdog a friendly pat on the shoulder, Hershel a hug and kiss on the cheek and Carol a tight hug.

Afterwards, we all seperated into groups. Carl and Beth were on opposite sides of our small camp keeping watch while the rest of us huddled over a map, deciding what to do next. I looked to Rick and nodded, signaling him to tell everyone about our previous find.

He cleared his throat and everyones heads turned in his direction.

"While me and Daryl were out hunting we found a secure prison. There are some walkers in it but we can clear them out easily." Eveyone nodded there heads in aggreement and we all spread into different cars, driving towards the prison.

Alyx followed me over to where my motorcycle was parked. She admired it for a moment before running her hand across the seat.

"You always wanted one of these..." She said, not making eye contact with me.

"and ye always wanted a ride on one." I finished her sentence. She nodded her head and stepped back so i could get one. She got on behind be and hugged onto my torsos tightly, resting her head against my back.

Alyx's POV

The rumble of the bike made me and Daryl's whole bodies vibrate. He kicked the kick stand and started to drive to bike in the direction of the prison.

I ran my hands up and downs his sides and across his chest. I slipped my hands underneath this shirt and rubbed his bare chest. I looked at his face to see he was clearly focused on driving. His jaw was clenched and his lips were in a straight line. He had a death grip on the handler bars and his knuckles were tiring white. I chuckled softly has I retrieved me arms from under his shirt and placed them on his shoulders.

I could tell he was turned on by my simple "friendly" gesture. Men are so weak when it comes to that stuff. They get tuned on so easily.

I leaned up and placed a soft kiss on his cheek before sitting back down and resting my head on his back.

We came to a stop in front of the large cement building a few minutes later. Daryl hopped of his bike and turned to me with a disappointed look.

"Don't do that kinda shit again, I almost crashed" He said with a chuckle. I smirked and stood up, placing a tender kiss on his lips before following the rest of the group towards the giant jail cell.

We all got out of our vehicles and made our way over to the outer fence. Rick handed Glenn some bolt cutters and Glenn cut a decent sized whole in the fence. We all scampered through the whole, Rick last so he could tie the gap back up with some rope.

"Okay, Daryl and Alyx go up in that tower." Rick ordered, pointing to one of the tall prison towers. "Hershel and Carl in that one" He said pointing to a different one. "Everyone else line up against the fence and distract the walkers while I run to the gate to latch it up."

he explained the plan furthermore. We all dispersed to our assigned spots as Rick got ready for his suicide run.

Me and Daryl jogged to our tower when he intertwined our hands and pulled me to him for a quick hug. He kissed my temple before pulling away and reloading his crossbow and my rifle. We climbed to the top of tower and exited the top door onto the balcony. We set up our weapons and gave a Rick a thumbs up, signaling we were ready.

Lori have Rick a small nod before she opened the gate and he ran out into the field full of walkers. I shot my rifle at any walkers that we're getting to close to Rick then I would like.

I heard the sounds of other people shooting the deceased corpse and the yelling of the people below us. Their screams wee getting increasingly loud and the walkers were thinning out.

Rick made it to the gate, he kicked a walker in the stomach and lathed the gate to the fence so it wouldn't open. He then ran to another prison tower and scurried up the steps.

"Light it up!" Daryl shouted to everyone, twirling his finger in the air. We finished killing all the walkers and a series of happy shouts echoed throughout the prison field.

--*

I am very sorry for not updating I'm so long, Christmaaasss is important ok

1)Is this their new safe haven?

2) are you happy with Daryl and Alyx's relationship?

3) Why hasn't Alyx told Daryl about what happened with her yet?

Twenty-three

7k reads?

Well slap me with a Canadian pickle and call me Esteban Julia Ricardo Montoya De La Rose Rameriez, that's amazing

Extra long chapter because why not?

Alyx's POV

We all entered the prison field with smiles plastered on our faces. I felt like I was finally home, finally back with my family. After being away from them for so long, this felt right.

Daryl positioned himself on top of an overthrown bus to keep watch while the rest of us built a small fire and made camp in the middle of the enclosed field. It was getting dark so we put out our sleeping bags and blankets to get ready for bed. I skinned a few squirrels for dinner and Carol cooked them on our makeshift fire. She filled bowls for everyone and we all dug in. I took two and easily scarfed down one.

"I'm gonna bring this to Daryl." I said, standing up and brushing the dirt of my pants. Rider nudged Glenn with a mischievous smirk on his face. Glenn took something out of his pocket and threw at me, I caught the small sliver packet with ease.

"Just in case." Glenn teased, wiggling his eyebrows. My cheeks flushed red as I looked at the condom in my hand.

"Oh Ha Ha, assholes." I shot back as I turned away from them and walked towards where Daryl was positioned. I heard them chuckle from behind me but I ignored the immature dickbags behind me.

When I reached Daryl I knocked on the bus and he whipped around, raising his crossbow. I put my hands up in fake surrender causing him to sigh and lower his weapon. He placed his crossbow on the bus roof and reached his hand down to help me up. I grabbed his hand and he pulled me up, causing me to stumble a few steps and almost fall of the roof. Daryl caught me though, and pulled me to his chest. I looked up at his crystal blue eyes and my stomach did flips. I would never get used to that feeling. His body radiated heat, making me never want to let go.

He lifted my chin up with his fingers and brought his lips to mine. The kiss was soft and slow, full of passion. When we parted, I was left breathless and my head was swaying.

I grabbed his face with both my hands and kissed him again, aching for his sweet lips on mine once again. I pushed on his his chest, not breaking the kiss but pushing him backwards so we walked towards the other end of the bus. He ended up leaning against the guard tower with me still snaking my tongue around in his mouth. He flipped us, so I was against the wall and he had trapped me in. I ran my hands down his face to the back of this neck to his broad shoulders.

We separated for a split second, just enough time for him to whisper in my ear.

"Jump" He mumbled rubbing his stubbly cheek against mine. I jumped and he supported my weight by my thighs as I wrapped my legs around his waist. We went straight back to making out, our body's presses together closer then I thought was possible.

He softly rubbed small circles on my thigh with his thumbs as I tangled my fingers in his light brown hair. I tugged on a few strands gently, making him moan against my mouth. The vibrations of his moan felt heavenly against my lips, I let out a quite moan as well. He moved one of his hands from my thigh to my butt, cupping it gently, making me moan again. A burning sensation started the grow in between my legs, we were both turned on by now. His lips traveled from my mouth to my cheek, jaw and finally landing on my neck. He sucked and lightly bit on the skin on my throat, making me bite my lip to keep from yelling. Every time he touched me I felt sparks shoot through my whole body. I felt the heat in between my legs grow even stronger but we couldn't do it right here, on top of a bus in the middle of a field, with the group only about a football field away.

I gently pushed his face from my neck, causing him to frown once I saw his blue eyes clearly enough. I shook my head and pointed to the group.

"Babe, we can't right now. We have to stop before I attack you in front of everyone" I said with a chuckle. He sighed and bowed his head before I untangled my legs from his waist and dropping them to the floor softly. I gave him one more kiss on the cheek and side stepped him to sit on the middle of the bus with my legs dangling over the side. I heard his footsteps come towards me and he sat next to me.

"The minute we're alone.." He mumbled, throwing his arm around my shoulder, sending the sparks through me again.

"The minute we're alone." I repeated pressing my lips to his hand for a quick second.

"So when ye gonna tell me wha' happened when ye were gone?" He asked, tilting his head to the side to get a better look at my face. I took a deep breath and closed my eyes for a second. I felt his warm lips press against my temple, encouraging me to start explaining.

"I took a walk and these assholes were trying to find the farm. I told them I didn't know where it was and I tried to get them to go away but they wouldn't... Carl told me you guys got one of them? Randall?" I asked. Daryl's whole body stiffened and he let out a shaky breath.

"Yeah, we got tha' one. He begged the whole time... Sayin' he didn't do nothin'... Sayin' he never hurt ye..." He mumbled. I rubbed his arm soothingly, getting him to calm down a bit.

"Did he tell you about me?" I asked, looking up at him but he didn't make eye contact, he just stared at the forest ahead of us.

"He told me tha' he found some cute tough girl in th' woods. I figured it was ye." He said, his mouth turing into a hard line. He looked down at me and nodded his head, telling me to counting telling him what happened.

"They took me...They beat me...I finally escaped after a few days and I went back to the farm but y'all were gone by then. I just hid out it houses and scavenged for supplies until I found y'all." I finished. Daryl looked a little unreadable for a second before realization and recognition covered his face.

"Those bastards beat ye?" He said in a low husky tone. I hesitantly nodded my head and waited for his outburst. It didn't come though. He just breathed harder then normal and blinked a few times.

"How?" He asked, his voice hoarse. I shook my head.

"Daryl you don't wanna know-"

"Show me" He demanded.

"Daryl.." I started. He shook his head and removed his arm from my shoulder.

"I need ye to show me, baby, please" He begged. I frowned and furrowed my eyebrows and scooted around so my back was facing him. I slowly lifted my shirt over my head and I heard him gasp. He looked at the slightly raised scars and I could almost hear his heart beat. The dark, long red lines showed brightly over the older pink ones. I heard a muffled cry and I turned back to him to find a few tears rolling down his face. I didn't even realize I was crying un till he reached a hand up to wipe away a tear.

He shook his head and looked at his hands in his lap.

"I promised myself...I swore I would keep ye safe. Tha' no one would ever do that to ye' again. Not after yer dad...not after mine ...M'sorry." He mumbled. I shook my head furiously.

"No no no no no baby...Its not your fault... They were all bad people Daryl, you're not like them. It is not your fault, I swear." I managed to say through the tears running down my face.

He nodded and I pulled my shirt back over my head before practically throwing my self in his arms and hugging so tightly he might burst. He rubbed my back soothingly as I laid my head on his shoulder and he wrapped his arm around my body. He buried his face in my dark hair and I felt his still falling tears dampen the top of my shirt. I let his even breathing and steady heart beat lead me into the best sleep I've ever had.

His arms were like a safety net, they were so protective and they felt like nothing could ever hurt me. For second that's what I believed.

--*Dream/flashback. *sexy scene beware*

19 year old Daryl threw his shirt into the growing pile of removed clothing along with his pants and underwear.

"I'll only do this if you want to." He said to the younger girl sitting a few inches next to him.

"I do. Do you?" 17 year old Alyx replied. Daryl hesitated before nodding his head. At first he was nervous about losing his virginity to his best friend. She was nervous about the same thing, but they talked about it, and there's no one else they would rather loose it to.

The both removed all their clothes and sat awkwardly next to each other. Neither of them knew what they were doing, Daryl has heard stories from Merle, but he never explained exactly how to do this.

Alyx made the first move, she kissed his lips lightly and he kissed back immediately, pushing his lips against hers. He gently pushed her onto her back, using his arms to support his self as he kissed her mouth and neck. They spent a good few minutes getting each other ready for what was about to happen. Kissing, biting, teasing and sucking until they agreed to do it for real. Alyx nodded her head, telling Daryl to start and prepared her self for the pain and pleasure that was about the come.

He lined himself up between her legs and entered her slowly. He cringed as he heard her muffled cries as she hid her face in a pillow. Once he was fully in he started to quicken his place and the pain started to fade. Moments later all Alyx and Daryl felt was pure pleasure. It was long, heavenly minutes of hushed words of love and the sound of bare skin on skin.

--*

I woke up on a blanket by the camp with Daryl's poncho thrown over me. I rolled onto my back and threw my arm over my eyes, shielding myself from the harsh light. I heard hushed voices from a few feet away and sat up to see Carl and Riley sitting together on the other side of the fire. They were hand in hand and whispering to each other. Both of them blushing majorly and awkwardly cuddling.

"What are you guys doing?" I asked. They shot apart and started to breath heavily.

"Um..Uh nothing" Carl spat out causing Riley to facepalm at his stupidity.

"Uh huh.." I sarcastically muttered as I stood to my full height and bushed the dirt off my pants. I searched the field for Daryl when I finally found his with Rick by the gate that leads into the prison. I started to walk on there direction where the dream finally hit me. It made me loose my footing but catch my self ungracefully.

I blushed thinking about the time me and Daryl lost our Virginities to each other. We said it was just to get it over with. There was no love involved. I think we were both lying.

--*

clears throat so uh.. that was my first time writing smutish stuff and uh.. it was really awkward..

1) Thoughts on this chapter?

2) How would you feel if I brought Dean and Sam Winchester in here? Just for fun?

3) Tell me your honest opinions on the sexy scene

Twenty-four

10k MOTHERFUCKER WHAT WHAT AMAZING HELL YEAH

Anyway, I went back to the very first chapters and I did some minor editing.

I love it when you guys vote for chapters, it makes me a lot more confident in my stories!

If it isn't asking to much could you guys comment more? I wanna see inside your brains! that's not creepy..

Alyx's POV

Today we were going to use the small group of fighters to clear out a cell block to live in. This 'team' consisted of Me, Daryl, Rick, Tdog, Rider, Glenn, and Maggie.

"We should have a group name" I said, to the group as we prepared to enter the Walker infested area. Rick and Daryl look extremely confused, while Tdog and Maggie looked down and smiled. Glenn, on the other hand, knew exactly what I was talking about.

"How bout... The fantastic four" Glenn recommended, putting his hands up as if the name was floating in the air.

"Glenn, there is six of us" Maggie said, placing a hand on her mentally unstable boyfriend.

"Yeah, I know. But that sound way cooler then the fantastic Six." He defended. I just shook my head and patted his shoulder.

"You're such a geek." I said under my breath as I walked away from him. He gasped and placed his hand on his heart, acting like he was offended. I just turned around and shrugged at him, earning a few chuckles from the fantastic four.

"Okay, ready guys?" Rick said as he placed his hand in the latch, ready to open it and unleash the flesh eaters. I looked at Daryl and he gave me a reassuring nod. I softly grabbed his forearm and leaned over to give him a kiss on the cheek.

"Let's do this" I said loud enough for everyone to hear. Rick unlatched the gate and walkers came flying out.

"Stay in formation!" Rick shouted as he sliced a walker head in half with his machete. I whacked away at the walkers until most of them were dead. We moved deeper into the yard and stopped when it was cut off.

"There." Rick said as he pointed behind a thick cement wall. We slowed tiptoed towards the destination when 2 walkers came out of no where. They were in full swat armor with helmets and everything. Daryl shot a bolt at one of them and it just bounced off the helmet.

"Shit" I mumbled as I ran towards one. I heard Rick and Daryl screaming from behind me but I ignored them and roundhouse kicked one of them in the head. The force of the kick knocked its helmet off so I stabbed it right in the forehead. I ran backwards to the group when I hit something hard behind me.

I turned around and was met with a very angry Daryl Dixon. I looked around to see that the other gate was closed and the rest of the walkers were dead.

"Were talkin' bout this later.." he whispered and turned away from me to follow Rick into the actual cell blocks. Aw shit. I'm in troubl e...

I ran after the rest of the group since they were already in the prison. I made a wrong turn and bumped into someones back.

"Oops, sorry Dar-" I looked up and didn't see Daryl's blue eyes, but unfamiliar deep green eyes.

"Who are you?" I asked the tall man with a cocky smirk, chiseled jawline and ruffled hair. I took a step away from him and lifted my machete. He removed a pistol from the back of his pants and pointed at the ground in front of me.

"Who are you?" He sassily replied. He had a flannel shirt with a worn out leather jacket, it looked like he's worn it for years.

I didn't get a chance to answer him because we heard a metal clanking coming from behind him.

"What was that?" I asked, trying to look over his broad shoulder and into the darkness, but still not taking my eyes off him. After Dave... I have to be even now careful with new people.

"Sam!" The man called out and seconds later another tall, but shaggy haired man nervously tiptoed out of the darkness.

"What? Oh uh, who is this?" Sam said, raising his pistol as well. The other guy looked at me, asking the same thing.

"I'm Alyx Johns... Who are you?" I answered, still not completely trusting the duo.

"I'm Dean Winchester and this is my brother Sam" Dean said, gesturing to the awkward brother behind him.

"Why are you here?" I asked, lowering my machete.

"Oh uh... We were just released when this started... We tried to help the others but we couldn't find them." Dean explained. Okay so these guys were just released from jail...Thats good to know.

"Okay, do you have a group?" I asked, still not trusting them completely. Dean narrowed his eyes while Sam tucked away his gun and smiled.

"No we don't, do you?" He asked.

"I do actually... But if you want to join it I have to speak with my leader first." I said, finally trusting them quite a bit "I have family in this group so I need to know you won't hurt them."

"We won't, I can promise you that. If my brother got hurt I would die so I know how you feel" Sam said, putting his hand on his brothers shoulder. Dean looked from him to me and then pushed Sam a few steps away so they could talk privately. Dean whispered something to Sam which made him make a very pissed off bitchy face. Dean saw the look and almost started laughing but Sam pointed in his face. The shared a few more words before coming back over to me and putting their weapons away.

"We'd like to join" Dean said, almost like he was forced to.

"Okay, follow me then." I lead them into the cell block where I saw the whole group frantically looked around.

"Stay here for a second" I told the brothers before I walked in and asked the closest person to me what was going on.

"Rider! What's everyone doing?" I asked the aggravated guy running past me. His head snapped up and he let out a deep breath.

"Guys! She's here!" He yelled out, cashing everyone to stop on there tracks and run up to me.

"Where the hell did ye go?" Daryl practically screamed. I put my hand on his fore arm to calm him down.

"I'll explain more later" I whispered to him. "Everyone, I-I found some people.." I started off with.

"What do you mean people? Like a small village?" Glenn remarked.

"You guys can come out now!" I ignored Glenn's comment while addressing the Winchesters. The two guys came walking out of the darkness. Dean, standing tall and strutting like he owned the place and Sam, almost like a mouse and scared of everyone in here.

"Who are they?" Rick asked, his face full of rage.

"This is Sam and Dean Winchester. I kinda ran into them before and they've asked to stay. You can interrogate them all you want." I told everyone. They all started barking questions and I quickly dashed out of the range of fire. I pulled Daryl into a cell and let him rant away.

"First of all, ye can't go runnin' off like tha' and puttin' yer ass in danger! Rick told ya to stay in fuckin' formation and ye just go out there and risk yer life? Didn't we jus' talk bout this the other night?

Stop tryin' to kill yerself!" He yelled, his face red in anger and his arms flailing around like a lunatic.

"Okay Daryl, I'm sorry that I ran off but I saw how the walkers where all geared up and it was an instinct, I'm sorry. I saw the opportunity and I took it. I was just trying to protect everyone."

"That's not yer job! How am I 'posed to keep ye safe when yer runnin' round like a dumbass!" He yelled. Did he just call me a Dumbass? He just unleashed a very unfiltered beast.

"I'm the dumbass? Mr. Ate-yellow-snow-when-Merle-told-him-to? I know you want to keep me safe Daryl, and I understand because I'm trying to do the same for you but I can take care of my self. I can make my own decisions."

"Yer right.. M'sorry. But what's with these two guys?" He said pulling me in for a hug.

"They seem okay, they said they were just let out of jail though..." I answered, laying my head on his shoulder. He nodded into my hair.

"Do ye think they killed 'um yet?" He asked with a chuckle.

"Probably"

*_*_*

Dedicated to LittleMrsUzumaki for giving me the idea to add Sam and Dean and dedicated to whatsup_itsmolly for giving my all the info on the characters

1) Sam? Like or naw?

2) Dean? Like or naw?

3) Someone pissed in Daryls cereal, is he over reacting?

Twenty-five

Alyx's POV

I balled my hands into fist and rubbed the sleep out of my eyes. I stifled a yawn as I looked at the gorgeous redneck sleeping soundly next to me. When I say sleeping soundly I mean snoring like a hog who overdosed on NyQuil.

I leaned over and gave him a kiss on the cheek before maneuvering my way around him without waking him. I silently hopped off the bed and quickly threw on a flannel and some jeans. Before I took of my shirt I checked outside the cell for anybody wondering around. When I found no one I threw off my grime filled shirt and replaced it.

I sighed in relief and walked out of the cell and downstairs to the common area. When I reached the door I reached for the keys and let my self in. Sam and Dean were sitting at a table with full bowls in front of them.

"Hey" San greeted as I walked over to them and sat down across the table.

"How'd the interview go?" I asked, with a chuckle, referring to the questions Rick asked them.

"Pretty bad, they hated us to much that they let us sit here with you right now." He said with a lot of sass and sarcasm.

Sam looked at him with his bitch face again and scolded him "Dean!"

Dean just shrugged it off and began picking at his oatmeal.

"Well, that's not the end of it" I informed, the group would throw another round of questions at them when they wake up.

"Can't wait.." Dean said under his breath. Sam rolled his eyes at his rude brother.

"Before the come in, I wanna ask some questions off my own." I said. Sam stopped inhaling his food, wiped his mouth and turned his attention to me.

"Are you guys good with weapons and such? We're supposed to clear out the rest of the prison later. Could you help?" I asked, tapping my fingers nervously on the metal table.

"If by good you mean totally badass, then yeah, we are pree-tty good." Dean said, putting emphasis on the pretty. I smirked as Sam, once again, scolded his brother. I chuckled but was interrupted when the sound of metal clanking against metal and footsteps echoed throughout the cell block. Seconds later Rick,Glenn, Rider, Maggie, Beth and T-Dog came storming in.

"Sup!" T-Dog said as he grabbed an apple off the table.

"Hey T" I called back. Glenn and Rider sat on opposite side of me, filling in the whole table.

"Introduce is to your friends, Alyx" Rider said, eyeing them suspiciously. I cleared my throat and shifted awkwardly.

"Sam, Dean these are my close friends Glenn and Rid-...Miles, this is Miles." I said. Rider hates being called by his first name, so I messed with him. When I said that, Rider turned to me and raised his eyebrow. Glenn stifled a laugh on my other side.

"Hi" Sam said, shaking their hands while Dean just grunted and continued picking at his food.

Glenn opened his mouth to ask a question when Ricks voiced boomed over everyone else's. I turned towards him and noticed that everyone else had filed in as well.

"Today, We are going to check out the new guys some more and then we will organize a team to clear out the tombs." He announced.

"The fantastic four!" Rider whispered in my ear, causing me to swat him away.

"Dean, Sam, We will ask you question which you need to answer truthfully, do you understand?"

"Yes, your honor" Dean said, comparing this to court. Rider almost laughed but I elbowed him in the gut. Sam just nodded, ignoring his brother.

"Have you killed walkers before?" They both nodded.

"Did you have a group?" They both shook there heads.

"Why were you in a prison?"

"Same reason as you" Dean said, lying because he told me what really happened before but I ignored it.

"How diverse is your stock portfolio?" Glenn asked from the corner. Some people on the group laughed, including Rick and myself. Rick shook is head looking down and then nodded.

"Okay, that's it... If you want to stay you can." Rick said, tapping on the metal table in front of him. Dean looked to Sam and Sam made puppy dog eyes and his brother. Dean rolled his eyes and then nodded.

"Yeah, well stay" He said. Sam elbowed him in the side. "and, we will help clear out the other cell blocks" He said, sounding forced.

*_*_*

Sam and Dean are staying! A woot a woot

1) How will everyone get along with the brothers?

2) why do I keep referring to them as the brothers?

3) so you want more action or romance?

4) do you like the new cover?

Twenty-six

Oh hot damn this is my jam bluhblujbluh till the am I don't understand make me wanna throw my hands in the air a-air a-a-air

If u type in Daryl Dixon in the search bar thingy my story is 50th...cool dude at least it's up there woo oh

*_*_*

"Okay, Me and Daryl will lead while Glenn, Tdog and Dean cover the back. Everyone else stay in the middle. Keep your guard up and and stay quite." Rick said as we assembled formation and prepared to enter the tombs.

Rick nodded to Carl and he opened the door, we all rushed in quietly. I walked in between Rider and Maggie, behind me was Hershel and Sam, then Tdog, Glenn and Dean. We all kept over weapons out in front of us, ready to kill anything that passed us. We tiptoed down the twisty hallways, stopping at each corner so Glenn could spray paint an arrow on the wall to help us get back. Each time the can rattled i silently cursed it out, being the only sound in the dark tombs.

We rounded another corner, Rick leading us through the death hallway. We shined our flashlights into the darkness, occasionally seeing a blood stain on the wall or a dead Walker on the floor. The rattling of Glenn's spray paint made me jump out of my skin and grab onto Riders fore arm aggressively. He winced and i silently apologized.

We walked for a few more yards in silence, and we could hear them...The groans.

Rick turned to us and pushed his finger to his lips. He continued forwards when the shadows of the undead danced on the cement walls. We focused our flashlights in the ceiling, to his ourselves from the walkers. They came at us anyway, and we killed them in an orderly fashion.

We thought we had it under control, but everything started to spiral. Another herd pressed through and the group for split in half. I looked around at who I was stuck with and I saw everyone but Maggie, Glenn, Rider and Sam.

"SAM!" Dean whisper shouted in the opposite direction. We shushed him and started to look around for our missing members.

I looked to Daryl pleadingly and he tiptoed over to me.

"We'll find him" He assured me in a hushed tone. I nodded my head, but I didn't fully believe him. This is my best friend, my brother and he's gone. He's lost. I couldn't take it.

"Miles Rid-!" I started to scream as a hand clamped over my mouth and shoved me against a wall. I closed my eyes and a single tear fell. I opened my eyes to be met with Daryl's beautiful blue ones. He looked at me with sympathy and concern as he gently removed his hand and placed it on the wall next to my head.

I closed my eyes again and took a deep breath. I wiped the stray tear and gave Daryl a kiss on the lips before squirming out of his grasp and strutting down the tomb.

I heard the footsteps behind me as my group followed.

"Maggie!" Hershel called in a hushed tone.

"Daddy.." Her faded voice echoed throughout the tomb. Hershel went in the direction of her voice, and in the process stepped over a dead Walker.

At least we thought it was dead.

The Walker awoke and grabbed his calf. It dug its teeth into his leg and took out a huge chomp of muscle and skin. He let out an ear piercing scream as I ran forward and lodged my pipe in its head.

"Daddy!" Maggie sobbed when she ran around a corner and at her bleeding father. She ran in our direction with Sam, Glenn and Rider close behind. Rider was losing the color in his face and he was dragging his feet, as am I. Dean ran to Sam and they gave each other a nod before turning back to fighting mode and standing back to back.

"Oh god.." I moaned as Rick and Daryl picked him up and dragged him down the hallway. I led the group through the tombs when we were cut off my a herd. "Turn around!" I yelled and shooting down a handful I walkers. The group readjusted Hershel and carried him in a different direction.

We came to a stop at a set of doors locked with a chain. I tugged in the handle and wasn't surprised when it didn't budge. I even tried kicking is when Daryl ran up and grabbed me by the waist, tugging me behind him.

"Stand back!" Tdog said as he shot at the padlock and kicked the doors open. We dove into the cafeteria and laid Hershel on the floor.

I searched the group for Rider when I spotted him holding his bloody arm and groaning quietly.

nonononononono NONO

"MILES!" I yelled when I saw the teeth imprint on his wrist, the the blood flowing onto the ground.

*_*_*

Daryl's POV

I was pushing as hard as I could on the door to keep in closed. My feet were slipping and the only thing keeping me from completely collapsing was the sound of Hershel's moans as they amputated his leg, and Alyx and Maggie's soft cries as they watched.

She's usually tougher then this and it looks like Hershel's gonna survive, what's she crying at?

"T!" I yelled at Tdog and in a second he was by my side, helping me keep the door shut.

"Step back" I warned and opened the door, releasing a few walkers into the confined space. I took down 2 and Tdog took down the last. I looked back at the group and Hershel's leg was clean off...Along with Riders forearm.

--*

I know this is extremely short but I really wanted to make it a cliff hanger I'm sorry.

1) will Rider survive?

2) I'm gonna start calling him Miles more idk it sound nice

3) Sam & Dean brotherly love, How are you liking them?

Twenty-seven

13k reads

a woah hoho damn

GET THE TISSUES

*_*_*

Alyx's POV

"Miles, Miles listen to me! You're going to be okay...You're gonna live..." I didn't even believe myself. I don't know if I was comforting him or myself.

He looked up at me from his position on the ground. He was on his back clutching the remainder of his arm, his eyes sad and glossy.

"I-I know..." He mumbled, the life slowly draining out of him. The tears kept coming, both of ours, pooling out of our eyes like a downhill stream.

He reached up and wiped a tear off my cheek.

"D-don't cry-y... Y-you... you said it yourse-self... Everything's going to be oka-okay"

*_*_*

Daryl's POV

"Duck" I informed Rick and stood up, aiming my crossbow at the 5 prisoners standing in front of me.

"Get them out of here" I growled at Rick, referring to the group, especially the injured ones.

I kept my crossbow raised as the prisoners stepped out. The leader, long hair, pulled a gun out of his belt.

"Who the hell are you?" I asked.

"Who the hell are you?" Long hair shot back.

"Why don't ya come on out of there?" I asked and they did.

"What happened to them?" He asked, looking at Rider and Hershel.

"They got bit" I answered and Long hair rose his gun.

"Woah woah! Easy now!" I said, aiming my crossbow higher and standing my ground.

"Who are you people anyway?" The guy with a mustache asked "don't look like no rescue team" He added.

"You got medical supplies?" Glenn asked, barging into there little area and looking for anything useful. The prisoners looked annoyed but they didn't do anything about it. He came back out moments later with a metal rolling table. They lifted Hershel onto it while Glenn and Sam supported Rider as he lost blood quicker and quicker.

The group ran out the door and I stayed behind, carefully watching the group of criminals.

Me and long hair glared daggers at each other until I followed after the group and back to our cell block.

We barged through the door and Rick started barking orders. Hershel and Rider got immediate medical attention and everyone else watched in suspense.

They are going to make it through that. I know they will.

Alyx came storming out, tears staining her perfect face. She ran straight for me and wrapped her arms around my waist, her face restating on my chest. Her tears moistened my shirt quickly, and i didn't mind. I rubbed her back in a comforting way and kissed the top of her head.

Her strangled sobs made my heart physically hurt. It hurts to see her like this, to see her in pain.

The footsteps of the prisoners echoed throughout the tombs as they nervously walked in the common room. I readjusted Alyx so she was still hugging me, but she was behind me, she was safe.

Long hair came in first, his pistol raised, then the big one, the scrawny one, mustache, and baldy.

"That's far enough" I said, standing up straighter and pointing my crossbow at long hairs face.

"Cell block C, cell 4, that's mine gringo. Let me in"He spat, waving his gun around.

"Today's your lucky day fellas, ye Ben pardoned by the state of Georgia, Yer free to go" I said, keeping my crossbow trained in the band of misfits.

"This is my prison! We're not leaving!" Long hair yelled.

"It's not yours" Dean said, walking in threateningly.

"Aye, it's Winchester! Where's yer puppy dog at?" Long hair barked, referring to Sam, I think.

"How do you know him?" Rick said, walking in as well, covered in blood.

"We were cell neighbors" Long hair said and Dean shook his head.

Rick just ignored it and looked back at the prisoners.

"A group of civilians, breaking into a prison you got no business being in? Why don't you take them to a hospital?" Long hair asked. While Rick explained that the are no hospitals, no army or government I whistled to Riley from the cell block. Her head popped out from a cell and she unlocked the door. I gestured for her come over here and she did.

"Take her away from here" I told the teen and unwrapped Alyxs arms from me. I kissed her head once more and the sight of her tear stained face made my blood run cold. I held in the tears as they two girls walked backed to the cell block.

Then I went back to arguing with the prisoners.

Alyx's POV

The pain

The sadness

The wondering

The emptiness I feel in my heart at the though of my best friend dying. His laugh, his smile, his everything... Just gone because of one flesh eating bastard.

This feels like a nightmare, a horrific nightmare that made its way into reality. And I can't wake up. This is real life.

This is real

I let out a agonizing scream into a pillow and shot out of bed. They told me to rest and try and sleep. How can I sleep at a one like this? When my brothers life is in danger?

I stomped down the stairs, constantly wiping stray tears from my cheeks. I passed the cell Miles was in and I collapsed In front of it.

People ran up to me, yelling my name, but all I could focus on was the slow rising of his chest as he inhaled and exhaled.

I Smiled and stood up, I ran to his side. I put my ear to his chest and I heard a heart beat, it was faint but God dammit, IT WAS THERE! I started to laugh, I was laughing but tears were still coming. I was happy but I was incredibly sad. He may be alive, but he is missing his arm. How can someone survive an apocalypse with one arm?

He can't. It encouraged my sadness. The horrible pain of knowing someone you love is going to die. Some day he is doing to die.

I looked at his chest and it stopped. The rising stopped. It stopped

Today is his day

He's dead

*_*_*

::(((

1) Sorry

2) sorry

3) how will she cope with this?

Twenty-eight

I would ride Miles Rider for miles ;)

Wait necrophilia...?

Daryls POV

I was keeping watch in the guard tower while Hershel and Rider were healing. I was repeatedly stabbing the cement wall angrily, thinking of the pain Alyx is going through. What am I doing here? Sitting here while she obviously need my support... I told her I would keep her out of danger, what the hell is wrong with me?

"Daryl! It's urgent.." Rick yelled as he ran through the doors.

"Wha's wrong? Is it Alyx?" I asked, the worry evident in my voice. He shook his head no and took a step closer.

"It's Miles...He's gone" He said, his voice cracking and his eyes turning glossy as years threatened to spill over.

I really thought he was going to make it through this... Maybe it was just too late.

"Okay... How's she Holdin' up?" I asked, pushing down all my emotions for right now.

"She's not... Go with her Daryl. I got this" He said and I immediately got up and sprinted to the prison.

I ran through the door and the first thing I saw was Dean sobbing in His cell.

"Dean?" I said, walking into his cell slightly. He quickly looked around and wipes his face.

"Yeah?" He said, trying to play cool.

"You hear about...?" I implied Riders death. He nodded and looked down.

"Yeah..I thought he was going to make it" He said clearing his throat.

I left him to cry over his fallen solider and I ran to Alyx and slid on my knees in front of her.

"Baby...Baby, come here" I said as I laid her down in my arms and rocked her back and fourth.

"It's okay...shhhhh" I soothed. She lifted her head and looked me straight in the eye.

"He said everything was going to be okay..." Her soft voice said before she exploded into more tears.

Alyx's POV

"There's so many things Miles was known for.

His sense of humor, his bravery, his selflessness, his dedication to helping other people when he needed help the most...

He was a loyal friend. There wasn't anything he wouldn't do for someone he cared about and that was one of his many amazing qualities.

I am going to miss how his eyes crinkled when he smiled or needed to give you really good advice. We can't really understand why he was taken away from us, and I thought about this all night because I want to know why someone so bright and happy is him is no longer here with us.

I know we all have great memories of times he made us laugh, or helped us. I think these are the best things to remember about him.

Today the sun shines through the field as we picture his sweet smiling face among the angels, no longer in pain. It is those left behind that must deal with the pain and loss we feel and while they are considerable, we can take comfort in knowing that he appreciated us.

When we remember what a fun person Miles was we can't help but smile, and as much as I am hurting today I know he is in a better place.Somewhere where he isn't afraid every second of every moment. He can finally relax after his long years at war and the years after he was fighting the undead beside us." Rick said, in the verge of tears as Daryl and Sam lowered his wooden coffin into the shallow grave.

My face is red and raw from the nonstop crying. The pain of this heartbreak is unlike anything I've experienced.

The whippings, the beatings, the torturing... It wasn't as bad as this is. This will leave the worst scar.

Rick took the small shovel and scooped up some dirt, gently placing it on top of Miles coffin. Glenn stumbled his way up after, tears escaping his eyes as well. One by one the group sprawled dirt on his grave until it was my turn.

My body was numb and I couldn't make it. I slowly made my way to his grave, my feet dragging against the soil. Daryl came and assisted me when I bent over to get the shovel.

My body physically hurt, it hurt to move, it hurt to think. Just picturing his smile broke my heart all over again.

everything's going to be okay

You were wrong

I stepped back and Rick proceeded to pile dirt onto the grave.

"Wait!" Riley yelled. We looked her confused. "listen" she whispered, putting her fingers to her lips and squinting her eyes.

"I hear it!" Beth exclaimed, searching for the source of the sound.

"What are yo-" Glenn clamped his hand over my mouth.

Thump Thump Thump

"Where is that coming from?" Lori whispered. I shrugged my shoulders. Carl ran up to Riders half filled grave.

"Carl!" Ricks scolded as his son started to removed the dirt from the hole.

"Carl stop!" I yelled, more tears coming as the boy destroyed my brothers grave.

"It's coming from here!" He yelled in excitement as Riley and Beth helped him dig.

What?

"It's coming from here! Come on help!" Riley yelled, throwing the dirt over her shoulder. Dean came over, his hazel eyes darker then I've ever seen. He wiped his eyes and removed the rest of the dirt.

Tdog handed him a crowbar and we all waited in anticipation as he removed the cover.

"Guys..." Dean said and swayed his hands in the air. We all walked forwards and looked down.

Miles was laying in his coffin with his eyes open and his heart beating. His mouth opened and I heard the voice I never though I'd hear again

"That was kind of rude, Don't you think?"

*_*_*

1) holy shit idk go crazy tell me ur thoughts

2) Dean/Miles ship name bc MOLLY told me to make them hook up and so I did

3) do you think it was stupid?

Twenty-nine

IM DILES AF

FOLLOW ME ON INSTGRAM @DAMNCHAN

Btw ARMS THO

*_*_*

Alyx's POV

We all just stared at our "dead" friend.

"How...?" I whispered as I clutched Daryl's arm tightly to keep my self standing. He grabbed my waist and held me up as we all silently stood their in shock. Dean was the first one to react to the "resurrection". He reached into Miles' coffin and picked him up by under his arms. Dean lifted him up so Miles was eye level with him and firmly connected their lips.

"What the hell is going on?" Glenn yelled, as the two continued making out. Daryl whistled and Sam rolled his eyes while muttering a 'finally'. The couple separated quickly and both of their cheeks turned bright pink. Dean put Miles on his feet and I took the opportunity to run straight at Him. I lunged into his arms and he stumbled a little before hugging me back.

"You asshole, I thought you were dead" I whispered in his ear as we rocked back and forth on our heels.

"I told you everything was going to be okay" he said back with a smirk.

"You are explaining the Dean thing later" I told him as I pulled back from the hug. He rolled his eyes and nodded.

"Nice eulogy by the way, Rick" Miles told Rick, giving his a firm handshake and a pat on the shoulder. Rick smiled and laughed, probably still shocked, as are the rest of us. Miles looked to Carl, Beth and Riley and the had a group hug.

"Thanks for digging me out of my grave guys" He said and we all chuckled.

"No... problem?" Riley said questionably. Miles continued to talk to the rest of the group and explain what happened when he was "dead".

"Let's get you inside" Lori said, putting her hand on his bicep and leading his into the prison, the group closely behind. Daryl and I strayed back a little bit and I intertwined my hand with his. I frowned and looked at the ground, thinking about Miles disability. It's great that he's back but he only has one arm, how will he survive like that?

"Aren't ye glad he's back?" Daryl asked me, knocking me off my train of though.

" I am... It's just... Nevermind" I said, shaking my head and clearing my throat.

"No, come on. Tell me" He urged me, giving my hand a squeeze. I sighed and gave in.

"I just don't know if he will live... He's only going to have one arm! Can he fight off walkers with one arm? He won't even be able to hold a gun." I said, my voice cracking.

"Alyx...Listen to me. He goin' ta be fine. If he can be buried alive, he can survive losin' a limb. He's a tough son of a bitch" He told me, chuckling at the end, I chuckled with him. I nodded and he kissed my cheek.

"Le's go" He said, tugging on my arm as we walked up to the prison with the rest of the group. As we made our what there, I looked over my shoulder at Miles' dug up grave and smiled.

--*

"So...You going to tell me about your new boyfriend or what?" I asked Miles as he sat on his bed and I stood in the doors way. He looked up at me and rolled his eyes before nodding his head.

"When the hell did it happen?" I started off asking as I sat with my legs crossed in front of him. He sighed and squeezed his eyes shut, thinking.

"Well I liked him almost right after he joined but, we didn't do anything until after I got my arm cut off." He said, I laughed and patted his knee.

"Okay, What's your favorite things about him?" I asked, I was actually getting into this. I know that teenagers talk about relationships a lot but I didn't really have a childhood, this was fun. He thought for a moment, smirking at me and rubbing his chin.

"Do I really have to answer this?" He whined.

"Unless you want a foot up your ass, then yes." I answered, pointing in his face. I tried to keep a straight face but I ended up bursting out laughing.

"Fine" He muttered. "I really like his voice and his eyes and his smile and his arms and that tough guy act and his humor and his bravery and his hella fine ass and..... Shit" He rambled on but stopped abruptly. I looked over my shoulder to see Dean standing there with a smirk on his face and a glimmer in his eyes.

"Oh so I'm just gonna go then" I awkwardly said as Dean walked closer to Miles and I could feel the sexual tension growing. I quickly got out of there and walked to my cell, smiling to myself. Miles was happy, so I was happy.

" Wha' ye smilin' 'bout?" Daryl asked as I walked into our cell and plopped next to him on the bed.

"Don't go in Miles cell for half an hour-ish" I said laughing. Daryl raised an eyebrow but I just shook my head and laid my head on his shoulder.I closed my eyes for a second and felt his warm lips touching my neck. They traveled up my neck, across my jaw and finally landed on my lips. Our lips connected and moved together in sync for a while until he pulled away.

"Ye remember when you said 'the minute were alone?'" He said in a low tone. I chuckled and nodded my head. "We're alone" He said and I immediately kissed him more roughly then before. He gently laid me down on the bed, our lips connected the whole time. His hands traveled down to the buttons of my flannel, where he carefully unbuttoned each one. He pulled it off while kissing down my neck and biting down softly on my collar bone. I gasped at the sudden wave of pleasure and tangled my fingers in his dark hair. He pulled off my shirt, and I did the same for him. He cupped my breast with one hand while the other pulled off my pants. He sat up for a moment so he could take of his pants and boxers, them my bra and underwear.

His mouth went back to work on my neck as he lined himself up in-between my legs and pushed in softly. We both moaned out in pleasure as he quickened his pace.

The rest of the night was the quiet sound of skin on skin and the recurring hushed words of love as we both reached our climaxes and fell into deep slumbers

--*

1) I tried to write porn I'm sorry how was it?

2) Is anyone else Diles af? I know Molly is

3) I'm kinda going of the TWD story line a little. Not a lot, just like timing and stuff. Is that okay?

Thirty

ITS 4 AM I DRANK 3 MONSTERS MY HEAD IS GOING TO EXPLODE

Alyx's POV

I woke up, tangled in the bed sheets and alone. Daryl wasn't next to me which got me a little worried but when I checked my watch, I realized it was almost noon. I quickly jumped out of bed and got dressed. I walked out of my cell and down to the common area where I found that nobody was in here.

"What the hell?" I mumbled, looking around for any sign of human life. I wandered outside and saw that Beth, Riley, Carl, Lori and Hershel were all sitting on the bleachers.

"Hey guys!" I waved to them, making my way over and plopping next to Carl.

"Good afternoon, Sunshine" Riley teased causing me to flick her forehead.

"Hershel you're looking good, ready to start running?" I joked. He chuckled and readjusted his crutches.

"Give me a day or two, I'll race you" he joked back. My gaze drifted to the outer field where Rick, Glenn, Dean, Sam, and Daryl were gathering fire wood from outside.

"Where's Miles?" I asked Carl who pointed to the right. Carol, Maggie, Tdog and Miles were moving around the cars.

"He should be resting" I said to no one in particular. Hershel nodded from my side and patted my back.

"Yeah he should, we told him but he is one stubborn boy" He chuckled as I did with him.

I looked out to the men on the perimeter and found who I was looking for. Me and Daryl's eyes connected and he smirked to me. I blushed and looked down, tucking a piece of hair behind my ear.

"WALKERS!" Carl yelled and my hand instantly flew to my holster where I pulled out my pistol and immediately started firing.

"Lori! Carl!" Rick yelled as he and the other guys ran to us. Maggie pulled Carl and Lori into the Prison while Riley, Beth and Hershel went up some stairs and into a fenced off area.

"Where are they coming from?" I asked Tdog, Carol and Miles, who ran over to me.

"Over there!" T said, pointing to a gate that was opened. He and Carol ran straight at it, firing at walkers in their path and stabbing the ones that were too close. I shot a few more before grabbing Miles only hand and dragging him in a different direction then the corpse.

"Alyx! Get outta there!" Daryl yelled as he impatiently waited behind Rick, unlocking the gates that were in their way. I looked to him and nodded, pulling Miles away from the walkers and into the prison.

"Over there" Miles said as he pointed at an open cell that we could run too without being eaten alive. We ran to it and I closed it behind us. The walkers chased after us and banged on the metal bars, begging to get in.

A loud, echoing siren started playing throughout the prison.

"What the hell is that?" I yelled at Miles, who shrugged and covered his ears.

We backed as far away from the door as we could and waited for any help. There was about a dozen walkers shoving their arms in between the bars and flashing us with their decaying teeth. I walked towards them and grabbed one of their arms, pulling hard and leaning forward to stab it in the temple.

"That could work" Miles said as he stood up and repeated my process. We killed about 2/3s of them when Daryl and Dean came barging in.

"Over here!" I yelled and their heads both snapped in our direction. They quickly killed the remaining walkers and looked at us with shocked faces. They worked together to drag the bodies out of the way and open the door.

I ran to Daryl and threw my arms around him, as did Miles with Dean.

"Who are we missing?" I asked Daryl as we continued to hug.

"Carol, Lori, Tdog, Carl, and Maggie" He said before he kissed my forehead and we separated. We walked back outside, hand and hand, where Rick, Sam, and Glenn all stood talking to Hershel, Beth and Riley about the missing people.

Daryl whistled to them and the turned around, when they saw me and Miles, the gave us small smiles.

"We found Carol and T, they're gone" Rick said, his voice cracking. "But that doesn't mean the others are too. Daryl you go with-" He started to throw around orders but he was cut off my the soft crying of a new born baby. We all slowly turned around and saw Maggie and Carl walking out of the prison. Maggie had a bundle in her arms... Lori's baby, but there was no Lori.

"Where...Where is she?" Rick stuttered, dropping his axe and wobbling over to his crying son. Maggie shook her head, tears escalating down her cheeks.

"Oh my god..." I whispered as a single tear fell down my face and Daryl pulled me to him.

"No, No...Aww no, Carl!" Rick yelled as he stumbled to his son and started sobbing. He fell to the floor and curled in a ball, crying loudly over his sobbing wife.

--*

They small baby's cries echoed as Rick got up from the ground and sat on his knees.

"Rick? Rick you with me?" Daryl said, waving a hand in front of his eyes. He stared off at nothing and swayed back and forth, panting heavily.

Maggie handed the small bundle to Carl who brought her over to Hershel.

"Let me see the baby" He said as we all walked over to him.

"Wha' we gonna feed it? We got any thin' a baby can eat?" Daryl asked Hershel worriedly.

"The good news is, she looks healthy, but she needs formula. And soon or she won't survive." Hershel said as he checked the baby over and over.

"Nope, not her. I'm goin' on a run, we ain't losin' no one else." Daryl said as he strapped his crossbow on his back and threw on his poncho.

"I'll back you up" Maggie's hoarse voice said from a few feet away.

"Okay, think where we're goin'. Hey Beth" Daryl said, pulling Beth to the side to talk to her quick.

"You two get the fence, too many pile up we got ourselves a problem!" He ordered Oscar and Axel, who obeyed quietly." Maggie! Le's go! We're gonna loose the light!"

I looked over at Rick and saw that he was sitting up and shaking his head. He slowly got up and reached for the axe he dropped previously. Rick ran back into the prison, ignoring our yells to stop him.

"Rick!" Maggie yelled but he ignored her.

I looked down at the small baby in Carl's arms and I patted his shoulder.

"You're a big brother now, how does it feel?" I asked him softly. He looked up at me with a smile on his face.

"Big brother Carl" He giggled and I flicked his hat. I gave him a small smile and turned back to Daryl who was packing his bike. I chased after him and grabbed both his shoulders.

"Listen to me, Daryl" I said to him, wiping my dry tears away. "I know it's just a little run, but you be safe okay? I can't take another death" I said, my voice shaking. He nodded his head and rubbed my arms soothingly.

"I'll come back, I promise" He said, walking over to his bike.

"I love you" I said, then realizing that was the first time I've said that to him.

"I love ye too" he said back, I could tell he had a smirk on his face just by the way he said it. He then talked to Glenn and Maggie about where they were going to find baby supplies. Daryl hopped on the bike and Maggie did behind him. Dean opened up the gate right before the drive through it, as did Oscar at the main one.

*_*_*

"They're back!" I heard Glenn yell from the guard tower as he kept watch. The sound of a motor got significantly louder as Daryl's motorcycle rode back into the prison. Carl, Miles, Hershel, Beth, Dean, Sam, Riley, the baby and I all sat in the common area, waiting for Daryl to burst through the door with formula in his hands.

The baby kept crying as Maggie and Daryl finally came inside with the supplies filling their bags.

"Beth?" Maggie asked, pulling her sister to the side to fill up the bottles with formula. I walked over their too and helped mix the water with the powder and create the liquid for the baby.

"How she doin'?" Daryl asked as he took off his poncho and kneeled by Carl who was holding the baby. He carefully took her from Carls arms while whispering comforting things in the baby's ear. Daryl rocked her back and forth, being the cutest little shit ever.

I handed him a bottle and he started to feed her it. After a few seconds she quieted down and drank the formula as Daryl fed it to her. I watched the way he held her so gently, like she was made of glass. He was meant to be a father, and a hell of a good one too.

"Come on, come on" He whispered, urging her to drink the formula. "She got a name yet?" He asked Carl who shrugged.

"Not yet but I was thinking maybe...Sophia? There's Carol to o...and Andrea, Amy, Jacque, Patricia or....Lori. I don't know" He answered, swallowing hard. I looked at him with sad eyes and patted his back, sitting next to him at a table. I draped my arm around the boys small shoulders and squeezed him gently. He looked at me with tears in his eyes and a sorrowful look. I leaned forward and kissed his freckled cheek causing his to blush a little bit.

Daryl continued to rock the baby and feed her the formula. "Yeah ...Ye like tha' huh?" He comforted the baby. "little ass-kicker? Right? Tha's a good name right?" He said and everyone chuckled. "Little ass-kicker, ye like tha', huh? Ye like tha' sweetheart?" He cooed and we all watched in admiration. My gaze was filled with love and care as I stared at the love of my life. I quickly snapped out of trance though, before anyone noticed. When I looked around the room I saw that everyone had there eyes glued to me, with little smiles on their faces.

*_*_*

I think this is the longest chapter I've ever written and that is very sad.

1) I like how this chapter went, did you?

2) Daryl is fricken cute as shit I can't breathe... Agreed? Jady if u say no I swear to god

3) Do u like Carl and Alyxs relationship? I do.

Thirty-one

Before you read this go read chapter 5 again. I did editing to it that is essential for this chapter. Go read it or part of this won't make sense!

Alyx's POV

"You were swooning" Glenn whispered in my ear as Daryl continued to rock the baby back and forth. I slapped his chest with the back of my hand and scoffed.

"Whaaat? I was not...You, uh, I-I, um... Look Glenny!" I pointed behind him and he turned around aimlessly.

"What?" He looked back at me and I flicked his forehead.

"Is that like your new thing?" He asked me, flicking my forehead back.

"Yes, which is why only I can do it" I said, flicking his again. He flicked me again, so I flicked him, so he flicked me.

"Enough! Children children, Please!" Riley scolded us as she stood on a stool to be our height. "As you can see, the redneck is really a big softie. We should savor this moment" She said, gesturing towards

Daryl and baby Grimes. "I know Alyx is" She mumbled to Glenn, expecting me not to hear.

I gasped and out my hand over my heart, pretending to be hurt by her sarcastic remark.

"Excuse you, Mrs. Carl Grimes" I teased, flicking her forehead. Her eyes went wide and she blushed while Glenn sniggered. We feel into a comfortable silence after that.

The whole night, Daryl wouldn't let anyone else hold the baby. Everyone went to their cells, except Daryl and I. He kept rocking the baby back and forth, shushing her and comforting her. He sat on the stairs with her asleep, tucked into his side.

"She likes you" I said, sitting next to him and laying my head in his shoulder.

"She's lil', She likes everyone" He mumbled.

"Sure, you big softie" I said, repeating Riley's words from before. He shot me a fake glare which made me laugh .

"Wanna put her to sleep now?" I asked. It was getting late and we should head to sleep too. He looked at me and nodded, we stood up and walked to Carls cell.

We looked in and saw Riley in their with him, they sat in the bed opposite each other. Carl leaned in, as did Riley but before they could kiss Daryl grunted. They instantly flew away from each other, Carl fell backwards and off the bed. He looked up at us and groaned, Riley blushed and got off the bed.

"Yeah, so Carl thanks for the comic book" She nervously said as she fled out of the cell. I laughed at Carls awkwardness as he readjusted his hat and cleared his throat. Me and Daryl had goofy smiles on our faces as we stood there with baby Grimes gurgling and making weird noises.

"I think she wants her brother" I said, poking her little nose. Daryl handed her I Carl and he cuddled her close to his chest. He gently placed her in the crib we made from old boxes and sat on his bed.

Watching Carl made me think of my brothers. I usually don't think about them, or tell anyone about them for that matter.

"You remind me of my brothers" I told Carl.

"You had brothers?" He asked, shocked that I've never mentioned them before.

"Yup, they were twins and they we're only half but I loved them just as much." I said. Daryl looked at me sadly.

"Do you know where your dad went?" I asked Carl as he took off his shoes and got settled in bed. He shook his head no and I sighed. I have him a kiss on the cheek and told him goodnight.

Together, Daryl and I walked back to our cell, hand in hand, to go to sleep.

"Watcha think in' bout?" Daryl asked as he laid down on the bed with one arm behind his head.

"Everything I guess. Carl and that baby need a father... I know why Rick is slipping its just not the best time." I mumbled, laying down beside him. He nodded his head and pulled me closer to his side.

"I love you" He mumbled into my hair as my back was against his chest.

"I love you" I answered back before drifting off to sleep.

--*

In the morning we all met in the common room. I took a seat next to Miles and Dean. They were in deep conversation so I turned to Carl who was sitting with his sister in his arms.

Daryl was outside paying his respects to the graves of our group members. When he came back we all sat around the room in silence. The only sound was the clanking of forks against bowls and feet shuffling against the concrete floor.

I looked next to me and Carl and noticed the look of sadness all over his face. He stared aimlessly at the dry cereal in his bowl as I rubbed his shoulder comfortingly.

Suddenly, Rick quietly walked in and went straight for his son.

"Rick! Rick...How are you?" I asked,jumping up and rushing to his side.

"I'm okay, I just came to see how Carl was doing" He said, patting his sons back and not even glancing at his daughter who was resting in Beth's arms.

"I cleared out the boiler block" Rick said.

"How many were there?" Sam asked.

"A dozen, two dozen, but I have to get back" Rick answered.

"We can take out the bodies" Glenn said, holding Maggie's hand tightly.

"No No, I have to do it" He said, "Everyone have a gun and a knife?"

"Yeah, we're running low on ammo, though" Daryl replied.

"Maggie, Miles and I were planning on making a run this after noon" Glenn said "Found a phone book, with some places we can hit, look for bullets and formula"

"We cleared out the generator room" Sam said "Axels there trying to fix it in case of emergency" He continued.

"Good, good" Rick mumbled brides tromping back into the dark tombs.

"Rick!" I yelled but he ignored me.

*_*_*

Me, Carl, Daryl, Dean and Oscar were looking through the tombs for any sign of Rick.

The floors were littered with dead bodies and blood splatters.

"Check it out" Oscar said as he aimed his flash light at a door. The door was opening and closing slightly every few seconds.

"Probably just one or two" Dean said as Daryl tapped the door and nothing happened.

"Don't look like they got much fight" Daryl said."They ain't goin' no where, we'll take care of it on the way back"

Daryl walked off, checking out the bodies while I strolled over to Carl.

"Come on" I said, patting his shoulder "You know, my mom, she was a really into cars, just like my old man. One day, I was about 5 and I was in the car with her when I started screaming about ice cream or some shit. When she turned to look at me, a huge truck slammed into our car and she was killed instantly. I was barely touched and helped out of the car but she was burnt down to nothing. That was the hard part, you know she's just gone, erased, nothing left of her. People said it was better that way, I don't know. Just made it seem like it wasn't real, you know? After she died my dad hooked up with some girl and they had my brothers, barely talked to them though"

"I shot my mom. She was out, hadn't turned yet. I ended it, it was real. Sorry about your mom" Carl said, tears in his eyes.

"Sorry about yours" I said back, rubbing his back with one hand. We both sighed and traveled deeper into the tombs.

We continued for a few minutes when Oscar shouted into a cell.

"Oh that's what I'm talking bout!" He said as he walked into a cell and came out with slippers.

"The hell you need slippers for?" Dean asked as Oscar bent down to pick them up.

"Ya know, then end of the day, relaxing" He said with a chuckle. A loud snarl cut him off and I spun around to be met with the hazy truss of a walker. All 4 of us shot at it and it fell to The ground with many bullet holes and an arrow in its chest and head. We all let out strangled sighs and I exhaled deeply.

"All right" Daryl said with a deep sigh. We looked at the Walker and saw that it had a knife impaled in its knife. Daryl bent down and pulled out the knife, which caused blood to gurgle up and squirt out.

"That's carol's knife..." He whispered.

We went back to the cell block and sat around the tables.

"I'll be right back" Daryl told me and he hurriedly walked back into the tombs

"Did you find him?" Hershel asked and we all shook our heads and plopped in seats. Beth was mixing some oatmeal in a big pot while Hershel rocked the baby in his arms.

Rick wobbled in the room, his eyes red and swollen from crying. He walked straight to his baby and stared down at her with a smile on his face. He took her from Hershel's arms and stared into her blue eyes. He smiled and let out a strangled chuckle. A tear rolled down his face and he cuddled her into his side, kissing her forehead.

Together, Rick, Carl, Beth, Hershel and I walked outside.

"She looks like you" Rick said to Carl with a chuckle. Rick looked off into the distance and he handed the baby to me. He looked into the distance again and this time I saw what he was looking at.

There was a dark skinned woman who was covered in guts.

*_*_*

1)I had to add the brothers, more about them will be explained later on

2) 19k???? SHIT IT MY EAR AND CALL ME SANDY

3) I'm in the mood to make covers, if u need one tell me.

Thirty-two

20k 20 FUCKING THOUSAND

SLAP MY ASS WITH AN ITALIAN SAUSAGE AND FIGHT MY BROTHER THAT IS AMAZING

in celebration, I will flow everyone who comments.

*_*_*

Alyx's POV

Rick and his gun at the woman. She touched her leg and brought her hand back to find that it was dripping blood. She let out a strangled sigh and started to walk backwards away from the walkers.

"Carl, give her to Hershel" I told Carl handing him the baby and running down the dirt path to Rick. The Walker started to smell the woman through her walker blood decoy.

"Should we help her?" I asked Rick as he continue to stare her down. She dropped her bag and hacked at the walkers with her katana. She fell to the ground in exhaustion and me and Carl shot at the Walker's strutting towards her. Rick ran through the gates and straight to the woman where he checked her for bites as Herschel asked previously.

"Gunshot wound" He said as he picked her up and threw her over his shoulder, carrying her unconscious body into the prison.

"Carl, get some water, Beth get a blanket and towel" He ordered. The two teens obeyed and rushed to get the supplies.

"She's not coming in the cell blocks" I said to everyone and they nodded in agreement. Rick took the water from Carl and gently poured it over her face and neck. She woke with a start and stared at us in fear. Se reached for her Katana but Rick quickly kicked it away.

"We're not going to hurt you, unless you try something stupid. What's your name?" Rick asked the woman. She didn't reply so Rick sighed. Behind us, the door opened and Daryl walked in.

"Who's this?" He asked.

"You wanna tell us your name?" Rick asked threateningly. She stayed silent which got us all aggravated. "You wanna tell us your name?" He asked again.

"Got something y'all should see"Daryl said as he gestured for us to walk into the cell block.

"We'll keep this safe and sound. The doors are all locked, you'll be safe here and we can treat that" Rick told the woman. She shot us a deathly glare and sighed deeply.

"I didn't ask for your help" She growled.

"Doesn't matter, can't let you leave" Rick mumbled as we all walked to where Daryl told us to and locked the door behind us. When we got to the cell, Carol was sitting on the bed.

Carol

"Oh my god..." I trailed off as I jumped forwards and pulled her into a hug. When I released her, Rick hugged her next.

"Thank god" He whispered as he brought her into a heart warming hug.

"Found her in a cell. Musta' passed out, dehydrated" Daryl told us.

She looked around and when she didn't see Lori she started to cry.

"Oh Rick.." She whispered, hugging him tightly. " I'm sorry"I looked to Carl to find he had tears in his eyes. He sniffled and wiped them away quickly.

"Hey, It's okay to be sad" He whispered as I bent down to his level. He just nodded and shook me off.

Carol walked towards beth, who was holding the baby in her arms. From the corner of my eye I saw the mysterious woman watching us from the common room.

--*

After our little reunion, Daryl, Dean, Rick, Hershel and I walked back over to the woman. She eventually told us her name which was Michonne.

"We can tend to that wound for you, give you a little food and water, then send you on your way. First you're going to tell us how you found us and why you were carrying baby formula" Rick asked her as she sat on a bench with a piece of cloth pressed against her bullet hole.

"The supplies were dropped by a young Asian guy, pretty girl and amputee" She said talking about Glenn, Maggie and Miles. I gasped and grabbed Daryl's fore arm roughly. He turned to me and gave me an 'you okay?' look. I nodded and released my death grip on his arm.

I just got Miles back, he can't leave again.

"What happened?" I asked.

"We're they attacked?" Dean asked, obviously worried about his boyfriend.

"They were taken" She growled.

"Taken? By who?" Rick asked.

"By the same son of a bitch who shot me" She mumbled.

"These are our people, you tell us what happened now!" Rick yelled as he grabbed her leg on the wound. She grunted and pulled away as Daryl raised his crossbow at her.

"Don't you ever touch me again" She yelled at Rick, pointing her finger in his face.

"Ye better start talkin'. Yer gonna have a much bigger problem then a gun shot wound!" Daryl said as he moved closer to her.

"Find them yourself" She growled at Rick. He stared at her and put his hand on Daryl's crossbow. Daryl dropped his crossbow as Rick told him too. Michonne glared daggers at us as we returned the favor.

"You came here for a reason." Rick said, staring as hard as he could at her. She avoided his glare and fidgeted in her seat.

"There's a town...Woodbury, about 75 survivors. I think they were taken there" She said.

"A whole town?" I asked.

"It's run by this guy, calls himself the governor. Pretty boy, charming, Jim jones type"

"He got muscle?" Daryl asked.

"Couple of military wanna-bees. Armed entries on every wall." Michonne answered.

"You know a way in?" Dean asked. She nodded her head.

"The place is secure from walkers but we could slip out way through" She snarled, furrowing her eyebrows. Rick nodded his head.

"Alright, you'll take us there. This is Hershel, the father of the girl who was taken. He'll stitch you up" Rick said. She nodded and Hershel began his work as we all walked out of the cell. We went our separate ways, Daryl and I went to our cell.

"We're going to get them right? I mean we have to" I nervously said as I paced back and forth on the cell.

"Yeah we are. There's no way in hell we're leavin' them" He mumbled. I sat on the bed with my head in my hands and I groaned.

"He can never just sit still and not get hurt" I said, referring to Miles. Daryl reached up and pulled my hands away from my face.

"If they're is one thin' I know bout him is tha' he can survive any thin'" Daryl said as he pressed a soft kiss to my forehead.

*_*_*

filler chapter ok but I wanted this to be up the day I got 20k

1) comment and I'll follow

2) THANK YOU FOR 20k ITS SO FLIPPING AMAZING

Thirty-three

I just started a Chandler Riggs fic make sure you check it out!

--*

"How do we know we can trust her??" Riley asked the group.

"This is Maggie, Glenn and Miles! Why are we even debating?" Beth said.

"We ain't. I'll go after them" Daryl volunteered.

"Well, this place sounds pretty secure. You can't go alone" Rick told Daryl.

"I'll go" Dean said and Sam nodded along with his brother.

"Me too" Oscar said.

"I'm in" I called out from the top Of the stair case where I was sitting. Rick glanced around at us and nodded.

"Daryl, Dean, Sam, Michonne, Oscar and I. That's who's going" Rick informed.

"What? No, I want to go too" I said, crossing my arms and standing up straighter.

"I know, we need you here, with the baby. We need you to protect everyone here" Rick told me, leaning in and titling his head. His piercing blue eyes caused me to shiver and I agreed.

As much as I would love to help save them, Rick was right. I needed to stay at the prison and protect the most vulnerable.

The group that was leaving was getting ready to leave. Daryl headed upstairs to our cell to gather supplies. I ran up after him and leaned against the cell door.

"Don't die please" I whispered. He turned his head away from his backpack and looked up from me. He walked over and pulled me to him. Daryl wrapped his muscular arms around my waist and I wrapped mine around his neck.

He used his thumb to tilt my chin up and placed a soft kiss on my lips. It was tender and passionate, our lips molding into each others.

"I won't. I love ye" He mumbled against me lips.

"I love you too"

--*

The group that was leaving was packing a car with supplies and backpacks full of weapons. I stood by Carol, who was holding baby Grimes.

By the car, Daryl was talking to Carl about something. I guess I was staring because Carol nudged my shoulder.

"He's going to be fine" She assured me.

"I know, he always is. Its Miles in worried about." I lied. Of course I was worried about Miles but I can't help but be worried for Daryl too.

"I'm sure he's okay too, He's tough" She said and I nodded as I walked over to the gate to open it for the car.

"Wasn't this place over run?" Michonne asked coldly.

"It was" I answered.

"And you cleared out all my yourselves?" She scoffed. " Just the few of you?"

"There were others.." I said sadly. She sighed and looked at the ground, regretting her tone of voice she used previously. I walked away, back to Carol and the baby.

"Carl" Rick said, getting his sons attention and pulling him around the corner to talk.

Daryl walked passed us and kissed my cheek. Once he noticed that Carol saw, his cheeks flushed and he cleared his throat awkwardly.

"Stay safe" He said to us both as he walked away. They all got in the cars and drove down the dirt path, out the gates.

As we were walking back inside Carl ran up to me.

"Guess what?" He asked excitedly. I chuckled and took his hat off, ruffling his hair.

"Me and my dad named my sister!" He said.

"That's great! What name did you pick?" I asked, laughing at his excitement.

"Judith Grimes" He said happily.

"That sounds like a great name"

--*

That evening, screams were heard throughout the forest nearby.

"What was that?" Riley asked nervously. We all shrugged and sat around the common room in an uncomfortable silence.

After we had a very unsatisfying dinner, we headed to our cells for bed.

"You are good with her" I overheard Axel say to Beth as I walked by. "You got little sisters?"

"No" Beth shook her head.

"How old are you anyway?" He asked her.

"17" Beth answered. I started to feel uneasy with Axel, he was hitting on a teenager.

"17, Interesting..." He said.

"May we speak with you?" Carol asked Axel. He got up, nodded and followed me and Carol into a different cell.

"What's the problem?" He asked like he wasn't just being a perv.

"Stay away from her" Carol and I said at the same time.

"Please" He said, looking over his shoulder.

"This isn't about you trying to repopulate the earth." Carol told him.

"I didn't mean no offense, I've been locked up a long time and, well, there weren't many women. you following me? I mean Maggie, she with Glenn, You're with Daryl.." He said pointing to me, "and you're a lesbian. I was just talking to her." He said pointing to Carol with time

"I'm not a lesbian" Carol chuckled.

"You got the...Short hair" He said, gesturing towards Carol hairstyle.

"I personally think that hair style suits her" I said, putting me elbow on Carols shoulder.

"You're not a lesbian?" He asked again as if Carol was interested in him at all. "My my, this is interesting" He muttered, looking Carol up and down.

"No it's not" Carol said walking off. I looked at Axel again and muttered 'Ew' under my breath.

Later that night, Beth and Carl were filling some guns with ammo.

"Finally got Judith to sleep" Hershel said as he rocked the little baby.

"How are we with formula?" Carl asked, worried about his infant sister.

"We have enough to last us another month" Hershel said happily.

"I'll take Alyx for some more at the end of the week" Carl said as he placed a pistol on a table.

"Your dad and the others will be back by then" Riley said, patting his shoulder from the seat next to him.

"We don't know that" He said sadly. "Right now, Judith is the only family I got..." Carl trailed off.

A loud scream echoed through the tombs, causing me and Carl to jump up.

"I'm going" Carl said, getting up and sticking his gun in his holster.

"I'm going with you" I told him and he nodded.

"I can't let y'all go down there" Hershel said, blocking out path with one of his crutches.

"My father would go" Carl said, cocking his pistol. Hershel nodded in defeat and Carl and I ran into the tombs with our guns ready.

We traveled down the dark hallways with our flashlights lighting up the path. A walker jumped out of no where and Carl quickly put it down.

He looked at me and I nodded silently before we made a turn into a big open area.

There was a screaming couple on the floor, a dark skinned man and a dark skinned woman hacking at the walkers with their weapons and two teenage boys guarding a smaller teen. The two fighting teens were surrounding the smaller boy and keeping the walkers of him.

Carl and I ran in, shooting walkers left and right.

"Come on!" Carl yelled, pulling my arm and calling the group of people to follow us.

"Hurry!" I yelled as we rushed down the hallways. The couple was slowing down and that's when I realized the woman was bitten.

"You have to leave her!" I shouted and the dark skinned man shook his head.

"No way!" He said, picking her up and throwing him over his shoulder. Carl shot at the walkers in front of us and we finally made it back to the cell block.

As we made our way back, I couldn't help but think that two of the boys were oddly familiar. I feel like I've known them for my whole life. They were twins, dark hair, dark eyes. One had his machete raised while the other towered behind his stronger brother.

"Oh god, Donna! Is she dead?" The man shouted at us. The dark skinned man places the woman on the floor while the lone boy sobbed.

"I'll take care of it" Carl mumbled, cocking his gun and placing it to the woman's temple.

"Whoa, whoa kid, wait a minute" The dark skinned man said.

"Carl, put the gun down" I whispered to him. He sighed and out his gun back in his holster.

"She doesn't have that long" Carl reasoned.

"Who the are you people?" The dark skinned woman asked. "How did you get in here? Who are you with?"

"Look we can help you, first things first" Carl said, eager to put the woman down for some weird reason.

"Carl, they can do it" I said to him, pulling gently on his arm.

"No Tyreese!" The man shouted. Tyreese covered the woman's face with a bandana and rose his hammer.

Carl and I walked to the door and went into the common room, locking the door behind us.

"Hey! What are you doing?" The dark skinned woman asked us.

"Did you just lock is in here?" Tyreese asked me and Carl who were joined by Beth and Riley.

"Open the door!" The woman yelled, banging on the bars.

"Sasha, Calm down" Tyreese said to his sister, I'm guessing.

"This room is secure, you'll be safe" I informed them as I walked away and up to my cell.

I heard the shouts of the new group but I tried to block them out. Laying on my cot without Daryl, it was difficult to fall asleep but I managed to.

*_*_*

Yay!! Tyreese!!

And other unknown characters *smirks*

1) what do you think of the new group?

2)Will Daryl leave with Merle like on the show?

3) ily Carl but he is getting kind of physcopathic (is that a word), what do y'all think?

Thirty-four

23k that's so cool guys lol thx sm ily didn't I get 20k like last chapter idek yall are pretty awesome tbh

3rd person POV

"Is this what you wanted? Is this why you killed her? You piece of shit daughter!" He yelled as he brought the belt down again and again and again... The small girls screams echoed throughout the small concrete room while the only parent she had left abused her.

Seconds later, the door burst open and a teenage boy ran into the room with a baseball bat in his hands.

"Daryl! Daryl please get out of here!" Alyx yelled as she pulled on the restraints that kept her in place.

A low chuckle escaped the fathers throat as he bent over holding his stomach.

"You think he's going to save you? This worthless redneck trash? He's just piles of dirt and cigarettes!" He said in a serious tone. He pulled a pistol from behind his back and aimed it at Daryl.

"Dad! Dad no!" Alyx begged, pulling on the ropes that were cutting her wrist. "Don't hurt him!"

"He's getting in the way" Alyx's father whispered as he pulled the trigger and sent a bullet into Daryl's lower stomach. The boy fell to the ground as a cry of pain softly filled Alyx's ears. She cringed and grasped the ropes tugging her away from Daryl.

"Stop! No please, I'll do anything... Don't hurt him anymore" She said, tears pouring down her face as she watched Daryl slowly bleed out.

"Don't hurt him anymore? I won't be the one..." Her father said, walking towards the same door Daryl came through and grabbing the handle. As he made his way over, he stepped over Daryl's limp body, kicking his side.

Alyx's dad opened the door and dozens of walkers came pouring in. They went straight for Daryl, ripping his flesh from his bones. He cried out in pain, whimpering and grunting while he laid there, helpless.

Alyx was sobbing, her eyes tightly shut closed, kneeled down because her knees couldn't handle her body weight at the moment.

"You bastard! He didn't do anything!" Alyx screamed, her voice cracking and her throat sore.

"He was your only friend, you don't deserve friends. He died because of you, add him to your list." Her father snarled as he walked up to her. He smacked her across the face, she barely felt the burning sensation in her cheek because of the pain in her heart.

"Please kill me" She whispered, lowering her head.

"My pleasure" Her father said as he took his gun and sent a bullet into his daughters head, ending her life once and for all.

I woke up in a pool of my own sweat and tears. My blankets were thrown all over the floor and my face was wet from excessive tears. I sat up and rubbed my eyes. I shivered slightly realizing I was only wearing shorts and a thin T-shirt. I grabbed a big jumper from my bag and pulled on a pair of socks.

I left my cell and walked down stairs, grabbing a cup and filling it with water, I sat at one of the tables. I listened to the silence of the night when I was interrupter by a soft clanking sound. Looking into the area where the new people were, I saw one of the twins gently hitting his knife against one of the bars on the door. I walked over and say across from him. He looked up to me with a surprised expression on his face.

"Hi" I whispered, sipping my water and leaning against the wall behind me.

"Hi" the fragile looking boy whispered. "May I have some water?" He asked sounding afraid. I nodded and handed him my cup through the bars. He thirsty drank all of the water and I softly chuckled.

"When was the last time you had some water?" I softly asked, looking into his dark eyes that were behind a pair of black glasses.

"2 or 3 days ago" he scratched his chin, looking introspective. I gasped and quickly stood up, grabbing a cup and filling it with some more water. I handed it to the boy and he drank all of it in a few big gulps.

"Thank you" He whispered, wiping his mouth with the sleeve of his striped sweatshirt.

"Do you want some food too?" I asked. He nodded furiously. I grabbed a can opener, an apple and a can of beans. He ate the beans and apple hungrily, finishing quickly and wiping his mouth again.

"Thank you, again." He squeaked. I nodded to him and rested my head against the wall.

"So what's your name?" I asked, opening my eyes and squinting at him.

"I'm Ethan Johns, and that's my brother Grayson" He said pointing to his twin.

Johns

That's why they looked so familiar, they were my brothers.

"Do you remember me? The last time I saw you was more then 10 years ago" I said, scooting closer and peering through the bars at him. He tilted his head and shook it.

"What's your name?"

"Alyx Johns" I answered. Realization covered his face and he sighed.

"Alyx! Oh my, your here!" He gasped and crawled to his brother. Ethan shook Grayson awake and Gray jumped up and grabbed his gun.

"What happened? Are you okay? Are you hurt?" He rambled, checking his brother for any injuries. Ethan chuckled and shook his head.

"She's here" Ethan said, nodding his head in my direction. Grayson looked at me and squinted his brown eyes. His mouth hung open in shock and his eyes went wide.

I grabbed the keys off the table and unlocked the door, they came running in and engulfed me in a hug. They were taller me, the top of my head right under their noses. I wrapped both my arms around the twins and hugged them tightly.

"You guys are so old" I said since the last time I saw them they were toddlers.

"We should say the same for you" Gray said jokingly causing me to playfully hit his shoulder.

*_*_*

Ethan and Gray are based off Ethan and Grayson Dolan and they are really hot tbh

(Grayson on left, Ethan on right in the pic)

1) where is Daryl like really

2) Will Rick accept the new people into their group?

3) Will Rick accept the twins into the group?

Thirty-five

1k votes omg guys that's so cool tbh lol ilysm

*_*_*

Alyx's POV

Later that night, I was trying to go back to sleep but I couldn't do it. The scene of Daryl getting ripped apart from my dream kept replaying in my head.

A few long hours later, the sun finally came up and the group started to wake from their deep slumbers. As I passed Carl's cell on my way down to the common room, I peeked in. Taking notice of the soundly sleeping baby beside him, I tried my best to be quiet.

I gently tiptoed over to him and poked his cheek. His eyes instantly flew open and he reached for his gun.

"Whoa whoa whoa! Easy there tiger!" I whispered yelled, chuckling as I put my hands up in fake surrender. He rolled his eyes but I could still see the faint smirk on his lips as he got up and out of bed.

Together, we made our way downstairs and grabbed some breakfast. The new people were sitting at the tables, eating and conversing quietly.

"We would love to stay, we can gather our own food and supplies" Tyreese said as he gently placed his bowl of beans on the table. Hershel looked at me as if he was asking what I thought. I nodded my head, saying that I wanted them them to live with us.

"We wouldn't mind, but it's not up to us. Our leader isn't here right now." He said calmly.

"When will he be back?" The other man, who's name I leaned is Allen said.

"We don't know, but soon. A large portion of our group is with him" I said, taking a seat in between Gray and Ethan. Ethan was indulged in a novel, while Gray was gazing at Beth. He lightly hit his shoulder with a small smile on my face. He quickly shook his head and rubbed his eyes.

"You like her?" I teased. He blushed a deep shade of red and awkwardly coughed.

"What? No, no way. I met her like yesterday" He rambled, all whole staring at Beth from across the room.

I was about to tease him some more when Riley walked in with Judith in her arms. The small baby gurgled as she pulled at Riley's dirty blonde hair.

Sasha looked surprised to see a baby and carefully walked over to them. She peered down at the new born and smiled.

"How are you?" She asked the teenager. Riley looked up at Sasha with a confused expression in her face.

"She's not mine" Riley said adding a soft chuckle at the end.

"Where's the mother?" Sasha asked. We all looked down and sighed. Carl wiped his eyes and shook his head.

"She didn't survive childbirth" Hershel said sadly.

"I'm sorry" Sasha said as she walked over to her brother.

"Man you guys have been through a lot" Tyreese said, looking around at us.

"Haven't we all?" I asked rhetorically. He nodded and sat down in front of me.

"What you do before this?" He asked, folding his arms and leaning on the table.

"US Army"I said proudly. His eyes widen a little and he smirked. "How bout you?"

"I was a Professional football player" He said. I chuckled and turned my attention to Hershel, who was telling everyone about something.

"You're the only decent folks we've come across in a long time" Sasha said, sighing and folding her arms.

"You've been out there all this time?" Hershel asked.

"We had this neighbor who was always preparing for the end of the world. He had a bunker under his shed. We stayed there for a while, until we ran out of supplies" He took a breath as if he was remembering something. "All these dead people walking around. It makes us living a little more like the living"

"Ben and Allen were the first people we ran into. Then Grayson and Ethan later on. They were with their dad, but he got separated" he continued.

My breath hitched in my throat and I let out a strangled cough. I stared at the twins with my eyes wide and my mouth open. Grayson and Ethan looked at me with their eyes gazed downwards. My heart started to beat two times faster and I placed my head in my hands. Letting out a deep sigh, I rubbed my eyes and shut them tightly.

"What?" Sasha asked as she noticed my sudden movements.

"Uh... That was my dad too" I trailed off, nervously looking at the shocked faces of the group.

"These are your brothers?" Carl asked, jumping up from his seat and rushing over. I nodded hesitantly. He smirked and plopped beside us.

"Cool!" Him and Riley said in sync. I grabbed a hold of Grayson's arm and quickly pulled him out of the common room and into a cell a little distance away from the group.

"Why were you with dad?" I asked worried. He rubbed the back of his neck and wiped his eyes where tears were starting to form.

"My mom left us a few years after you left and we had to move in with him" he said sadly at the mention of his mother. I put my hands on his shoulders and peered into his deep brown eyes.

"Did he...h-hurt you?" I hesitantly asked. A few tears built up in his eyes as he nodded. "Ethan...?"

He shook his head furiously. "No, no I had to protect him. I had...I had too" he muttered. I squeezed his shoulders and pulled him to me. I rested my head on his shoulder and squeezed his torso. I heard his quiet sobs fill the cell as he let his sadness and anger towards our father out.

"It's okay, he's not here anymore" I said and he buried his face into my long dark hair.

"I love you so much Gray"

He nodded and cried harder into my neck, wetting my hair and shirt with his tears.

Thirty-six

I'm tired so this may have spelling errors and such dont judge <3 l

*_*_*

Daryl's POV

"It won't work" Rick said.

"Its gotta, Look, th' governors probably on th' way ta the prison right now. Merle knows how he thinks and we could use th' muscle." I said, tyring to persuade Rick to let Merle stay at the prison. It turns out, Merle was the one who took Glenn, Maggie and Miles. I'm not sure if Alyx will forgive him for that.

"You really want him sleeping in the same cell block as Carol? Beth? Alyx?" Glenn said. I froze when he mentioned Alyx, how can I just leave her?

"He ain't a rapist!" I exclaimed.

"Well, his buddy is.." Glenn trailed off, giving Maggie an uncomfortable glance. She twiddled her thumbs and looked at the ground.

"They ain't buddies no more, not after last night" I said, remembering when The Governor forced Merle and I to fight to the death. He punched me a few times before we fought our way out together.

"There's no way Merles gonna live there without putting everyone at each others throats." Rick said, placing his hands on his hips.

"So you're gonna cut Merle loose and bring th' last samurai home with us?" I said, gesturing to Michonne.

"She's not coming back" Rick defended.

"She's not in a state to be on her own." Maggie said.

"She did bring you guys to us" Miles said.

"And then ditched us" Rick said, rasing his voice slightly.

"At least let Hershel stich her up" Miles said.

"She's too unpreditcable" Rick spoke.

"Tha's right, we don't know who she is. But Merle, Merles blood." I said, turning the conversation back to Merle.

"No, Merle is your blood. My blood, my family is standing right here and waiting for us back at the prison" Glenn shouted, throwing his arms around in crazy gestures.

"And you're part of that family" Miles said, staring straight at me. I avoided his intense gaze and shifted my crossbow on my shoulder.

"But he's not, he's not"Rick said. I glared at him until he was forced to break eye contact.

"Man, y'all dont know!" I shouted, angrily. I stormed towards the car. "Fine, we'll fend for ourselves."

"That's not what we're saying!" Miles argued.

"No him, no me" I grumbled, looking over my shoulder as my brother was coming back to conciseness after being knocked out by Rick.

"Daryl, you don't have to do that" Maggie said.

"It was always Merle and I before this." I said.

"What about Alyx? I thought you guys grew up together?" Miles asked angrily.

"Man, that's different. Alyx...She'll understand." I said, my voice becoming much softer as I thought of her.

"You serious?" Glenn said. "You're just gonna leave like that?"

"You'd do the same thing" I spat, venom lacing my words.

"What do you want us to tell Alyx?" Maggie said. I looked down at my feet. It hurt to leave her but she would do the same thing if it were her brother, right?

"She'll understand" I repeated.

"Daryl stop!" Rick yelled, chasing after me as I walked to me brother. "We need you at the prison, we need to to help protect what we have!"

"No him, no me" I said again. "Tell Alyx I said M'sorry"

Merle threw his arm around my shoulder as we walked into the forest. After walking fora few minutes, realization hit me.

"I can't believe I did th' for ye'" I muttered.

"Come on little brotha'! Why ye need those pussies anyway?" Merle said as he pushed me roughly.

"Alyx is with 'um!" I shouted angrily. His face dropped and he frowned.

"Le's go get 'er then" he suggested.

"Man, ye jus' don't get it! She won't leave 'um! I love 'er and ye had to come and fuck everythin' up!"

"Love? Baby brotha', did I lose my hand so ye could love some tramp ye picked up?" He snarled.

"You lost yer hand 'cause yer a simple minded piece a shit!" I growled, pushing him and storming forward. Merle grabbed the back of my shirt a ripped it in half. With my shirt missing, my scars were revealed.

"I-I didn't know...he..?" Merle stuttered. I held back tears as I stood up and picked up my shirt.

"Yeah, and he did the same to ye'" I said, pointing in his face with an arrow. I started to walk in the opposite direction of him and he whistled.

"Where ya goin'?" He shouted.

"Back where I belong." I muttered as I walked farther.

"Ye can't.. I can't go with ya!"

"Ya know, I may be the one who's walkin' away, but yer the one who's leavin'" I said before leaving him behind and going back to my family.

*_*_*

This is a v short chapter

M'sorry

1) Daryl's going back?!?!?

2) how will alyx react when she realizes he left in the first place??

3) will alyx forgive Merle?

Thirty-seven

I wanted a really sad pic of her but i couldn't find one Bc this actress is so happy and adorable uugghh

--*Alyx's POV

"They're back!" Riley yelled from her cell as she gazed outside. My feet carried me through the cell block and into the court yard.

Glenn drove a green car through the gates first. Stopping in front of us, Maggie, Dean, Miles, Michonne and him hopped out. There was another car behind then, which I assumed Daryl, Sam, Rick and Oscar were in.

My eyes lite up once I saw my best friend step out of the car and slowly jog towards me.

I ran towards Miles and threw myself into his arms. He wrapped his muscular arms around my waist as I hugged his chest tightly. I tested my head on his shoulder and signed deeply.

I pulled back and I looked up at his injured face. He had a black eye, a long bruise on his cheekbone, his lip was slit and bleeding, the collar of his shirt was ripped and covered in blood.

"Who did this to you?" I asked angrily, through gritted teeth. Miles looked around at Glenn and Maggie, almost asking for permission to speak. They nodded hesitantly and Miles grabbed both my shoulders with his large hands.

"Merle was at Woodbury. He beat me and Glenn for answers on where we were camped" He said slowly.

My face started to heat up with rage. My vision blurred and was replaced with red. All I could see was red. My nostrils flared, my eyes flashing and closing into slits. I closed my hands into fist, my face turning purple as I became enraged.

"That bastard" I muttered under my breath. Miles put his hand on my shoulder to try and calm me down. I quickly turned and pushed his hand off me. I sighed and rubbed my temples.

"Just tell me where Daryl is" I said, once I noticed that he didn't come out of the car with Rick. Neither did Oscar. "Is he..." I trailed off, tears forming in my eyes. Miles quickly shook his head.

"No, he's okay. He left with Merle, he said you would understand" I sucked in a breath and closed my eyes.

"When will he be back?" I asked calmly. Miles sighed and looked at his feet.

"We're not sure if he will come back at all" He said sadly. I sighed with my head in my hands. I physically and emotionally felt my heart break as my eyes widened.

He left

He just fucking left

I felt as if my whole world was crashing down right it front of me, piece by piece, and all I could do was watch. I started to walk back into the cell block when I broke into a sprint and raced back into my cell.

I heard my name being called but I ignored it as I stopped in my cell doorway. I placed my hands on the sides on the doorway and bowed my head. Little tear drops fell down my face and hit the cement floor. The cell block was so quiet, I could hear every time a tear dropped.

I broke down on my bed and curled into a ball, resting my head on my knees as I cried and cried. The tears creeped down my face, one after another, soon it turned into a flowing stream of sorrow. I had wiped my face so much that it was red and swollen. I went to look around but my vision was blurry; it was difficult for me to see clearly. The sadness I felt was unbearable.

My whole body tingled and my head pounded. The sadness was eating me alive, from the inside out.

Miles' POV

As hours past, Alyx never left her cell. She was a wreck. After locking herself in her cell for hours, the sound of wailing and suffering still echoed throughout the cell block. No matter how many times her brothers and I knocked on her door, she wouldn't open it, and her sobbing was preventing her from speaking through the door.

When she finally emerged, she looked no calmer than she had when she'd received the news. Her face was dripping with saltwater despite her trying to dab her face with a rag, and moans escaped her lips through the suppressed sound of hiccups.

She slowly walked down the stairs and to the common area. She called out for Grayson and Ethan who appeared at her side instantly. She simply stood on her toes, kissed their foreheads, grabbed a cup of water and headed back upstairs. Her cries soon echoed throughout the cell block once again.

"What happened?" Ethan asked me and Grayson nodded along, asking the same thing.

"Do you guys know Daryl?" I asked. They thought for a second and the hesitantly nodded.

"That was the guy she was always with, right Gray?" Ethan said.

"Yeah, the Dixon kid" He replied.

"So he went to be with his brother and left Alyx behind. They were really close, like in love close" I said sadly. The teenagers nodded their heads understandingly and walked off to do their own things.

Rick walked by with his head bowed and hand on his gun.

"Rick, what are we going to do about the new people?" I asked. He looked over my shoulder at the small group of people and sighed.

"I don't think they can stay" He said, rubbing his eyes.

"You're gonna kick them out?" I asked, surprised. He nodded while scanning the room, squeezing his eyes shut every now and then.

"You can't kick those twins out, they're Alyx's brothers. She's already lost enough" I said. He hesitantly nodded.

"They can stay, but the rest have to leave." He ordered. I nodded and walked over to them to announce the news. Tyreese and Sasha stood up with frowns on their faces.

"What did he say?" Sasha asked.

"He said you have to leave, except Grayson and Ethan, they stay"

Sasha gripped her brothers fore arm and furrowed her eye brows.

"W-we won't be a problem... Please" Tyreese pleaded.

"It's not up to me" I said.

"We can gather our own supplies!" He shouted.

"It's not up to me!" I said with more anger then last time. Some people backed away in fear. "I didn't mean to snap... Its not up to me. Rick!"

Rick came in seconds later and explained it furthermore. He started to yell and wave his gun around, yelling at them to "get out". The thing was, he wasn't looking at them as he said it. He was looking at nothing, just thin air.

--*

Idk how to end this

Happy Easter

1) Is Rick going crazy?

2) How did you like Miles POV?

3) the Easter bunny is a lie

Thirty-eight

Alyx's POV

I didn't want to leave my cell. I didn't want to see or talk to anyone. I just wanted everyone to leave me alone so I can be sad in peace.

Many different members of the group came up to me to bring me food or water. They slid a tray towards me and I would retrieve it after they left. I wrapped myself up in blanket and rested my head on my pillow.

My whole body hurt to much to move. I was suffering and Daryl caused it. I love him and he did this to me. Does he love me back?

"Alyx, you need to eat" Grayson said as he walked into my cell with a tray of food.

"I'm not hungry" I lied and covered my head with my blanket. My stomach growled, loudly.

"I know you're lying" He said, chuckling. I ignored him and buried my face deeper into my pillow. "He's not worth it"

"What?" I lifted my head and glared at him.

"Daryl. He isn't worth this, all this crying and hiding away. You should let him go. Hell, you should be mad at him for leaving" He said, sitting down on the bed next to me. "Do you love him?"

"Yes!" I snapped.

"Does he love you?" He asked. I didn't answer because I didn't know the answer. I used to think he did, but now, I'm not sure. He wouldn't leave someone he loves, right? He loves Merle and he is with him right now.

Grayson could sense how unsure I was. He rubbed the back of his neck and scooted closer to me. He quietly leaned over and planted a kiss on my forehead before getting up and leaving the cell.

I groaned and threw the blankets covering me to the ground. I marched out the cell and downstairs. I could tell everyone was surprised to see me up and moving but I ignored their stares.

"Where are you going?" Dean asked as I grabbed a sniper rifle and a machete from the table.

"Out" I muttered angrily, stomping out of the cell block. Axel opened the first gate for me and then Glenn did the main one.

"Are you coming back?" Glenn asked, his voice shaky and unsure. I didn't verbally answer, but I gave him a small nod and stalked into the woods in my own.

A small herd of walkers was stumbling towards me after I walked for about a mile.

"He isn't worth this" I muttered, tears escaping my eyes as I ran towards the walkers.

"He isn't worth this" I said again, pulling out my rifle and aiming at one of there heads. I pulled the trigger and watched the brains and blood escape the walkers head.

"He isn't worth this" I repeated, shooting down 2 more walkers. I pulled out my machete and sliced through the heads of a few walkers. I kicked one down by its leg and stomped on its head while shooting down another. I ran towards one and jumped in the air, harshly bringing down my machete on its decaying skull.

I finished off the last few walkers and sat on the ground with them around me. I folded my legs and let more tears fall from my pale face as I repeatedly stabbed the dirt beneath me.

Yes he is

The stupid, asshole redneck I fell in love with was worth every second of pain and sadness. I can't stop loving him so I all I have to do is wait for him to love me back. At least come back...

After a few more hours of staring off into space and absentmindedly playing my my machete, I heard rapid gunfire coming from the prison. I jumped up and sprinted in the direction of the prison nonstop.

There were unfamiliar trucks surrounding the gates with rifles, shooting at my group.

I snuck up behind one man and held his head back by his hair. In one swift motion, I snapped his neck and stole his gun. I jumped into one of the cars and killed the driver with my machete. There was a pile of grenades and other explosives in the back seat of the car that could come in handy. I took a couple grenades and hooked them to my pants securely.

I got out of the car and shot down a few more men and women on the opposing group. I continued to shoot down people while honking the car horn with my foot.

Many of the nearby enemies heads turned towards me with there guns raised. I unhooked a grenade and threw it in their direction, earning screams of terror.

I ran far away from the on coming explosion and ducked behind a tree. The car blew up and killed several men and women.

I was bragged harshly by a mystery man from behind. He leaned close to my ear and whispered words I never wanted to hear.

"How's my daughter doing?"

I pushed his arm up and brought my elbow down on his stomach. He bent over in pain and coughed up some blood. I faced him and kicked him square in the jaw, knocking him out cold.

A bullet was shot in my direction and I looked over in the direction it smell from. A tall man with an eyepatch was shooting directly at me. I ran as far away from the rest of the men and women as I could. In the distance I saw my group in the prison yard, shooting at the opposing group with the little ammo we had.

Those bastards smashed through our gates and let dozens of walkers into the field.

As I was making my way around the gates to go into prison through a back entrance, I thought about the man who claimed to be my father. He looked a lot older then I remembered, but he had the same devilish grin and hateful eyes.

It really was him.

It was my father.

--*

Whoa whoa whoa

Short chapter, I know

1) How will everyone react to Alyxs Father?

2) What should his first name be? I haven't decided

3) What will gray and Ethan think of their fathers return?

Thirty-nine

3 2k+

HOOK UP WITH RANDY AND FUCK A BABY SEAL THATS AWESOME

*_*_*

Alyx's POV

As I jogged up the field and up to the prison, I slashed at walkers with my machete, left and right. I was getting tired but I fought on. Once I made it to the top, Grayson opened the gate and let me inside.

"Hey Gray" I said, pulling his in for a small hug. He looked down at me and nodded his head.

"You're good?" He asked, checking my arms for bites. I nodded and squeezed his forearm gently. Glenn drove a truck threw the gates, with Michonne and Hershel in the back. Hershel hopped out and hugged his daughters lovingly. Glenn got out and stood over by the side, watching his girlfriend. I walked by him and stood by his side, my arms crossed. I looked at the ground and tapped my foot against the pavement.

"He's coming back, you know." Glenn said from beside me. I looked up at him and frowned.

"I'm not sure I want him to." I said, my voice breaking. I used to think I loved Daryl, so so much. Now that he left me, without saying anything, my feelings changed. He really hurt me and I can't forgive him. If he came back, it would pain me to look at him.

"What? Why?" Glenn asked. I sighed and bit my bottom lip.

"It would kill me to look at him. After what he did... I'm not sad anymore, I'm just very angry." I said, spitting out the last word. Glenn was about to speak but something behind me caught his eye. His jaw dropped and he cleared his throat.

"Um, Alyx?" He said, pointing behind me. I raised my eyebrows and turned around, not expecting what I was about to see.

"Alyx!" Daryl shouted, running towards me. He tried to throw his arms around me but I pushed him back.

I don't know what I was feeling. Definitely not happiness or joy. It could've been anger but mostly betrayal. I felt betrayed. I brought me hand up and slapped him across the face.

"Don't touch me." I growled.

I pushed his shoulder to the side and walked inside to prison, letting tears fall from my eyes and land on my shirt. I passed everyone who tired to talk or touch me.

Once I made it to my cell, I kicked the wall, hard. My foot throbbed but I ignored it as I kicked the walk again. And again and again. The toe of my boot was scuffed so I started to punch the wall instead.

I was sobbing, throwing punches at the cement wall, angry with Daryl and myself.

Rough hands grabbed my wrist and pulled the from the wall. Daryl pulled me to his chest and wrapped his muscular arms around my waist. I hit his chest but he pulled me to him tighter. I eventually gave up and rested my head on his shoulder, uncontrollably crying.

"Alyx stop. Look at me." Daryl said, pulling my chin up with his thumb and pointer finger. "M'sorry, I need ye to list-"

I stepped back, angrily throwing his arms away from me.

"You're sorry?" I let out a short laugh but my smile disappeared as fast as it came. "I don't care if you're sorry, leave me alone! You've hurt me enough! How could you just leave me like that? I trusted you, I loved you!" I shouted, tugging on the roots of my hair and passed back and forth.

"Ye' did th' same!" He yelled. "Ye think I wanted ta leave ye? Ye know how many times I thought' bout ditchin Merle an' comin' back to ye? No ye don't, 'cause ye didn't listen to me."

"I did not do the same!" I barked, pointing in his face, hurt that he would even say that.

"Yes ye did! Back when we were lil'. Ye left to get outta yer house. Ye were too scared ta' stay wit' yer dad. Ye' jus' ran away an' left me behind! Like you didn't care, like you wanted to get away from me." He shouted, his voice cracking near the end. He bowed his head and rubbed his eyes. "Maybe I coulda done somethin', somethin' to keep ye from leavin'... I-I didn't know why, I didn't understand... I said I did, I should've said somethin' else... somethin' ta' keep ye from leavin' me."

I brought my hand to my forehead and sighed. He should have said something. He should have told me to stay. I would've...

I know how he feels know. He felt like trash, like his dad always told him. He felt worthless, like no one cared about him, not even me.

"Daryl stop. I would've stayed... I would have. But I didn't. And you felt like garbage, I know that because that's how I feel right now." I said, looking up into his glossy blue eyes. Little tears fell from his eyes, but not as much as mine. He nodded and tugged at his hair.

"M'sorry" He whispered.

"I'm sorry too" I whispered back. We stood there for a few minutes, just looking at each other. Eventually, one of us pulled the other towards them, and we ended up in a solid embrace. I pulled back and wiped the tears from my cheeks.

"We should go make sure Merle isn't harassing anyone." I said, starting to walk out of the cell.

"Ye know he already is, righ'?" Daryl said. I chuckled because he was probably right.

"Yeah.." I nodded as we walked down the steps. Daryl bumped my hand with his lightly and I felt the goosebumps I always gets when he touches me. I think I do still love him, but does he still love me?

He laced our fingers together and brought my hand to his lips, where he kissed me softy. He let go as we got outside to see the group huddled around Merle.

I remembered what he did to Miles so I charged forwards. I tapped on Merles shoulder and he spun around quickly.

"Aye! Girlie, how ya-" I cut him off with a hard punch to the nose. He fell back, holding his face as blood began to drip.

"Y'all ain't gonna do somethin'?" He yelled to Rick and Daryl. Rick looked at Daryl with his eye bows raised.

"Ye deserved it." Daryl said and Rick agreed. We walked back inside, the group as a whole, and into the common room. We all took a bowl of some beans and rice Carol had cooked up and sat down at the tables. It felt like we were a family, eating together at the dinner table.

Carl sat down next to me and ate his food quietly.

"Why did you leave?" He asked, not looking up from his bowl.

"I had to take care of some things." I answered.

"Like my dad did after my mom died?" He asked, looking up at me sadly.

"Kind of..." I trailed off, finishing my food and heading upstairs, Daryl trailing behind me.

I sat down in the bed to change and take off my boots. Daryl leaned into the wall from the doorway, watching my every move.

"Watcha' doing there, Pervy?" I teased, throwing a shirt on.

"I love ye, ye know tha', righ'?" He blurted out.

"You still do?" I asked, sitting back on the bed.

"I never stopped"

--*

HA GAYY

1) When will Alyx tell Daryl about her dad?

2) will we see her dad again?

Forty

Alyx's POV

My feet buried themselves in the white sand with each step. The waves crashing down on the shore, the seagulls flying above, the happy screams of children running around.

My hair flew in the wind, dark sunglasses in front of my long lashes and deep eyes. Eyebrows neatly tamed and skin surprisingly clear.

The sky bright blue, dotted with cotton clouds and the ordinary shining sun.

He walked up to me, taking my hand in his and swaying it slightly as we walked together. Ray-bans covering his eyes as well and a loose button down dangling from his broad shoulders.

I brought out hands to my lips and kissed the back of his softly. He stopped my from walking any further and pulled off his raybans.

His stunningly blue eyes contrasted with his tanned skin as he squinted at me. A small smile was evident on his face as he took both my hands in his.

He took a deep breath and closed his eyes. He opened them seconds later and sank to one knee.

"You're the most bad-ass, fierce, stubborn and defensive woman I've ever met in my life. You're also the most caring, charming and hilarious woman I've ever met in that same life. Luckily for me, I've gotten the chance to meet you, even though the circumstances were horrible, and make you the biggest part of my life.

The first thing you ever did to me was kick me out of my seat at the school lunch table. Then you became the boss, and I was okay with it. You arranged the play dates and when we were doing this and how we did that. You helped me, with homework, my dad, Merle and anything I needed you for. I can't repay you for that.

Remember when we were 15, I got beat so bad I couldn't move or sleep or talk? You stole your dad's truck and drove me out far away to fix me up. You cleaned me and fed me and did everything for me for almost a month. Then when I was strong enough, we drove back and no one noticed I even left. But people noticed you. Especially your old man. He did stuff to you that weren't even close to what my dad did. You suffered through all of his shit and didn't tell him where you went. He starved you for days until you told him and you never did. You were so strong. You are so strong. I can never repay you.

I've asked for everything there is from you. I've asked for advice on shit like school and girls and even cars because you knew everything about all that stuff. I just want to ask you for one last thing and then I'll do everything. I'll do anything and everything for you because I am so madly and deeply in love with you.

So, Alyx Presley Johns, will you marry me?"

My eyes fluttered open slowly as the sun shone in through the windows. My arm draped across Daryl's stomach, our legs intertwined. I was extremely comfortable and didn't want to move but I really had to pee.

I gently lifted my arm of the rednecks chest and used my other arm to support all my weight as I hovered over him. In one swift motion, I was off the bed and Daryl didn't notice. I smirked to myself as I tiptoed through the cellblock until I found the bathroom. I wandered in and saw the empty showers and thought 'why not?'.

I finished my business and turned on the shower head. Clear water shot out and steadily fell to the floor. I smiled triumphantly as I stripped my dirty clothes and stepped into the path of the water. The water was cold, but it still felt amazing after not having access to clean water for so long.

I washed as much grime and blood off my slim body as I could. Removing about 4 layers of it, I was satisfied and hoped out.

I forgot about towels. I groaned in frustration as I walked aimlessly around the bathroom, looking in closets and cabinets for anything to dry me.

The sound of the door opening scared me. I jumped and ran behind a trash can nearby.

"God dammit, you scared the shit out of me." I said to Daryl as he smirked at my naked body.

"Keep that smirk off your face, Mr. Pervington." I teased with a chuckle. He pulled something from behind his back and threw it at me. I caught the blanket with ease but instead of wrapping myself in it, I rolled it up and slapped Daryl with it.

"What- Ow!" He said, flinching as I hit him repeatedly. "What are ye- stop!" He shouted.

He grabbed the towel and pulled me with it. I tripped but Daryl caught me and pulled me towards his chest.

"This ain't what I came down 'ere for but-" He started to say but I cut him off my connecting out lips in a passion filled kiss. Our lips moved together, mesmerized lips against mesmerized lips in a fiery heat.

Our hands traveled around each others body's, mine ending up in his hair and his on my back. He ran his fingertips down my spine, making me shiver under the touch.

--*

oh god oh god oh god so ok

I didn't have a phone until May 30th.

I then went on a cruise June 1st

I got back yesterday

Im posting this now

I hope yall are good and happy (I added sexy time for youuuu)

Forty-one

Alyx's POV

"What are we gonna do now? The Governors been stalking us, keeping us from leaving. He's gross and I hate him. When I was at Woodbury, you wanna know what he said to me while I was bleeding on the floor? You wanna know? He said, 'looks like you need a hand'. Are you freaking kidding? I'm the only one allowed to make amputee jokes about myself. I'm outraged. Frustrated. This is ridiculous. How are we gonna get food and water? We're just gonna rot here? Until he gives up?" Miles ranted. He paced back and forth in his cell, running his hands through his mop of brown hair.

I sat on the bottom bunk with my legs crossed and back against the wall. I had a book in my lap, The Passage by Justin Cronin. The cover was worn out and wrinkled, pages crinkled and ripped, the black cover hanging out by bits of tape. I was over half way through when Miles snapped his fingers in me and Sam, who was seated next to me, faces.

"Are you listening?" He asked. I answered without taking my eyes off the paper.

"Yup, Stalking, basic necessities, rotting bodies, I hear you." I said. Sam hummed along, as he was engulfed in a book as well. Something about mythology.

Miles sighed and sat down on the bed across the room. He sighed and groaned, leaning his head on the wall behind him.

We sat in silence for a few minutes, I kept reading as he sat across from me. He was staring, impatiently tapping his leg with his fingers. He groaned again, rubbing his eyes with his fist balled up. I looked up from my book to find him staring at me again.

"You wanna do something?" I asked. He nodded his head eagerly.

"Go run some laps, kill a baby cow, find the cure for cancer."

"Find the cure for this infection." Sam suggested.

"Yes, listen to demon boy." I said.

"Maybe he should Just stop sitting her like a toddler who didn't get to go outside for playtime." Sam continued.

"That sounds like a fantastic idea." I took a deep breath and rolled my eyes. "Go!"

He dashed out of the room and down the stairs.

"What are you doing?" I heard Glenn ask.

"Running laps!" Miles answered, his voice fading as he ran farther away. I laughed to myself and continued reading.

Hours later, I heard footsteps coming towards my cell. Carl ran in, covered in sweat and dirt.

"What's up, bud?" I asked causally.

"Andrea's here." He said. Sam looked at me with his eyebrows raised. I put my book down, grabbed his wrist, and raced out of the cell.

*_*_*

"Where's the rest of you?" Andrea asked. "Shane?"

We all shook our heads.

"Lori?" She paused, seeing us all lowering our heads. "Rick... Carl." She gave a sad look to Carl, who wiped his eyes and broke eye contact.

"Alyx?" She searched the crowd until she spotted me. She let out a sigh of relief, since I was missing when she got separated.

"This is where you all live?" Andrea asked. We all nodded quietly.

"Can I go in?" She asked, wandering towards the door.

"I won't allow that." Rick said, stepping in front of Andrea.

"I'm not the enemy, Rick." She defended.

"You say that now, but just days ago your boyfriend ran through our fences with a dump truck and shot us up." I budded in. She turned to me and gave me a dirty look.

"He said you fired first." She said, looking surprised.

"Well he lied." Daryl grumbled from across the room. There was a small pause before she started speaking again.

"I didn't even know you were in Woodbury until after the shootout! I came as soon as I found out."

"That was days ago." Glenn said, rolling his eyes.

Michonne, who had been lurking around the room while Andrea was talking, stepped forward. She leaned against the wall, a smug expression written clearly on her face. Once Andreas attention turned from us, Daryl took a seat on the table next to him. Slowly, I side stepped and sat on the chair next to him.

"What have you told them?" Andrea questioned Michonne.

"Nothing." She replied smoothly, shrugging her shoulders nonchalantly.

"I don't get it." Andrea started to explain her self. "I left Atlanta with you people and now I'm the odd man out?"

I bit my lip and clenched my fist at my sides. She was pissing me off.

"The Governor almost killed Michonne and he would've killed us." Glenn said, starting to explain. Andrea cut her off, lifting her hand towards Merle.

"With his finger on the tigger! Isn't he the one who kidnapped you? Beat you?" As if giving up, she covered her her mouth and shut her eyes tightly. "Look," she continued, dropping her hands, " I cannot excuse or explain what Phillip has done, but I am here trying to bring us together. We have to figure this out."

"There's nothing to work out." Rick soar harshly. "We're going to kill him. I don't know how or when, but we will."

From the corner of my eye, I could see Miles smile, but quickly cover it up with a cough.

"We can settle this." Her voice sounded pathetic and defeated. "There is room in Woodbury for all of you."

"Over my dead body." I muttered quietly, so no one could hear.

"For the first time since Andrea arrived, Merle opened his mouth, probably to spit a nasty comment at someone.

"Ye should know betta than tha'." I was surprised when no insults left his mouth, but also extremely relived.

"What makes you think this man wants to negotiate?" Hershel said. "Did he say that?"

"No..." Andrea said, bowing her head. I heard a scoff from behind me. Probably Dean.

"Then why are you here? If he didn't send you here, maybe your just making everything worse!" Dean was fed up. This really isn't his place to be talking, but he was right, so we let him continue.

Andrea scowled at him. "These people are my friends." She said, gesturing to all of us. "I was with them much longer than you have. I came here to tell you that he's gearing up for war. The people are terrified. They see you all as killers. They're training to attack."

"Tell you what..." I said. "Next time you see Philip-"

"Tell him we're gonna take his other eye." Daryl finished my sentence, throwing me a reassuring glance and nodding his head.

"We've taken his shit for too long. If he wants a war, he's got one." Glenn threatened.

Andrea turned to Rick with pleading eyes.

"If you don't sit down and try to work this out, I don't know what's going to happen. He has a whole town. Look at you." She threw her arms in the air. "You've already lost so much. You can't stand alone anymore."

"Watch me." I mutter, standing up and walking out of the common room and outside.

*_*_*

hello my naughty children it's murder time

Forty-two

49k!!!!!!

GO SCUBA DIVING IN BERMUDA AND SHOVE A CANDY CANE UP MY ASS

THATS AWESOME

So I'm trying out 3rd person point of view writing tell me if u like it

*_*_*

"Is she gone yet?" Alyx's usually rough and demanding voice was soft and quiet. She sat comfortably in the corner of her cell bunk bed, legs bent and pulled to her chest. A new book open in her lap, "Evermore" by Alyson Noël.

Daryl stood by the entrance, using one arm to support himself against the door frame. He tilted his head, raised an eyebrow and blew out puff of air.

"Lef' a few mins' ago." Daryl announced, taking a seat at the end of the uncomfortable bed. He rested his elbows on his knees, head in his hands. Alyx bent the edge of the page she was on, and closed the book.

"You okay?" Alyx asked, crawling towards Daryl and sitting on her knees beside him. He rubbed his eyes and nodded. By the look on his face, Alyx could tell something was wrong. His eyebrows were furrowed, lips curled down and body stiff.

She raised her eyebrows, not believing him. He sighed and leaned his back against the wall.

"Jus' stressed, tha's all. 'M good." He said. Alyx wrapped her arm around his shoulder and played with the ends of his brown hair.

"What do you thinks gonna happen? With the governor and all." She asked, staring at his face, taking in every detail she could see. The only light source was the moon shining in from the barred window, which didn't give much.

"He's gonna do somethin' bad. He's gonna take somethin' or someone. He'll probably try an' attack us." Daryl answered. He turned and looked at Alyx, first at her eyes and then down to her lips.

"Do you think Andrea can help?" She questioned, scooting closer to the redneck beside her. He scoffed and shook his head.

"Nuh uh. She'll try, an' he'll shoot 'er down. Was never a good plan." He leaned his head back against the wall and stared up at the ceiling. "She's gonna get 'erself killed. An' then all of us."

Alyx let out a soft hum and rested her head on her shoulder. "We'll be okay." She said softly. She said this is for the benefit of both of them. Neither really believing it though.

"Let's go to sleep." She suggested, earning a quiet grunt and nod from the tired Daryl beside her. She kicked off her boots, as did Daryl, and the crawled underneath the blankets together.

He laid his head down on her chest, instead of how they usually do it reversed. He found it comforting, while Alyx enjoyed the warmness he seemed to radiate.

"I love you." She said.

"I love ye." He replied.

*_*_*

Alyx woke with a start. She had a horrible dream, but couldn't seem to remember what it was about. The only thing remembered were four words.

I can show you

The two words held much meaning, but Alyx didn't know it. She rubbed her eyes and gently moved Daryl's arm from her body. She sat up, stared into space for a few seconds before getting up and walking out of the room.

The cells were dark and quiet, everyone still sleeping soundly. She tiptoed down the stairs, making quiet creaks and silently cursing every time she did so.

She got into the common room without waking anyone and sat at one of the tables.

"Why are you up?" She heard a voice ask. Alyx looked up and saw her younger brother seated a few feet away.

"Couldn't get back to bed. You?" She asked Grayson. He sighed and took a sip of water from the cup in his hand.

"Ethan was kicking in his sleep and it was really annoying." He said. Alyx let out a soft chuckled and stood up from her seat. He nodded his head in her direction, telling her to take a seat next to him.

She did so, laying her head against the younger ones shoulder.

"Are you scared? Of the governor?" He timidly asked. She looked deep into his dark brown eyes, which resembled her own.

"No. He can't do much unless we are scared. He's like dad. He'll use our weaknesses against us. Don't let him scare you. Everyone in this group is your family, we will protect each other. We will be okay." She said, rubbing his back lightly. He nodded his head and let out a buff of air.

"Ethan can't do it anymore." Gray said, mentioning his twin brother.

"Do what?" Alyx questioned, tilting her head to the side.

"Survive. This is all too much for him to handle. I'm trying to keep him safe, keep him alive. But I don't know if I can do it much longer. He's weak, he needs to be strong. Like us."

"Grayson. Ethan is strong. He is a different kind of strong. You're physically strong, which keeps you alive, but he's mentally strong. That will keep him alive." Grayson nodded again and looked at the cup of water in his hands.

"He doesn't know." Gray said.

"Know what?"

"About dad. About how he was sick and twisted and liked to be the biggest asshole of a father."

"He doesn't know?" Gray shook his head.

"If Ethan did something bad, I would take the blame. I would tell him to go outside while dad did it. I wanted to make sure he never had to experience what we did." A tear rolled down his cheek as he spoke about his father. "Every time. Every single time. He called me a coward and useless. I was trying to save Ethan! But dad just kept saying it. He would give me double the beatings if I protected Ethan. He told me that Ethan would grow up to be a baby and never know how to take care of himself. Know Ethan's gonna die because I didn't teach him how to live."

"None of anything he had ever said to you is true. He was manipulative and sinister. He was a drunken bastard who didn't give a shit about his kids. I swear Gray, nothing he has ever said to you, will ever be true."

*_*_*

ITS SHORT AND BAD BJT I WANT IT UP RN

Forty-three

Are u kidding me

52 THOUSAND Reads

actually ridiculous

like what

I'm 10 I don't deserve this have any of u read this story it's crap are u kidding

Thank u u stupid babies

iu

*_*_*

Alyx's POV

We all sat around a small lantern in the middle of the cell block. I sat on the stairs next to Carl in a comfortable silence.

All of our minds were full of crazy thoughts about what the Governor was going to do next. The silence was broken as Rick walked down the stairs with a sleeping Judith in his arms.

Beth took notice in the baby as she squirmed in Ricks arms. She started to sing a soft melody and keep the beat by tapping her thigh.

"They hung a sign up in our town, If you live it up you won't live it down"

I smiled at the music, since I haven't heard much in a while. Beth had a beautiful voice that gave a happy feeling to all of us.

"So she left Monce Rio, son. Just like a bullet leaves a gun"

I slowly stood up and walked over to Daryl, who was leaning against on the cell doors near the exit. I stood next to him and leaned my head against his shoulder, listening to the soft lyrics being sung.

"With charcoal eyes and Monroe hips, She went and took the California trip"

Rick walked towards us with Judith, no longer squirming, but snoring quietly. The baby started to resemble her parents more and more each day.

"Well the moon was gold and her hair like wind, said don't look back now. Just come on, Jim."

Merle wandered in from his cell and threw me a dirty look, that I certainly repaid. I don't remember what we fighting about, but it was probably nothing that big. He seemed annoyed by Beth's singing, but I still thought it was beautiful.

"You've got to hold on, hold on. You've got to hold on. Take my hand, I'm standing right here, you got to hold on.

Well he gave her a dime stone watch, and a ring made from a spoon. Everyone's looking for someone to blame, if you share my bed, you share my name."

Daryl gestured towards Rick has he sat down beside us.

"Some reunion, huh?" He said. Rick scoffed and nodded.

"Well go ahead and call the cops!"

"She's in a jam." Rick said, slowly rocking his baby back and fourth.

" You don't meet nice girls in coffee shops"

"We all are." Hershel said, looking up at us from a stool he sat on nearby. "Andreas persuasive. This fellas armed to the teeth. Bent on destruction."

"She said baby, I still love you. Sometimes there's nothin left to do"

"So what do you wanna do?" I asked Rick.

"We match it. I'm going on a run." Rick told us.

"I'll head out tomorrow." Daryl volunteered.

"No you stay here, keep an eye on your brother."

"Oh you got to, Hold on, hold on, You got to hold on. Take my hand, I'm standing right, here, you got to. Just hold on"

"I'm glad you're back, really, but if he causes problems, it's on you." Rick told Daryl.

"We got him." I told Rick, who nodded along.

"I'll take Michonne." Rick said.

"You sure that's a good idea?" Daryl asked.

"I'll find out. And Carl. He's ready. Alyx, you wanna tag along?" I nodded immediately. "Alright."

"Well, God bless your crooked little heart St. Louis got the best of me. I Miss your broken-china voice,. How I wish you were still here with me"

"You hold it down here." He said to Daryl and Hershel.

"You got it." Daryl said confidently.

"Well, you build it up, you wreck it down. You burn your mansion to the ground. When there's nothing left to keep you here, when. You're falling behind in this big blue world

Oh you go to Hold on, hold on, You got to hold on. Take my hand, I'm standing right here you got to hold on"

--*

Carl, Rick, Michonne and I left before sunrise. We each carried all we had. I had a machine gun and a small knife, Carl had his gun, as did Rick, and Michonne had her sword.

We got into the blue Hyundai, me and Carl in the back, Michonne driving and Rick in the passenger. As we drove down the road and out of the prison gates, I stared out the window. The song Beth was singing got caught in my head and I was softly humming the melody.

Carl looked at me and tapped my leg.

"Shut up." He whispered.

"You shut up." I whispered back. He furrowed his eyebrows and turned away, probably annoyed with how immature I was.

A man with a bright orange backpack was running down the road next to us.

"Help! Please don't leave!" He shouted. Neither Rick or Michonne acknowledged the man while me and Carl turned to watch his as we passed.

"No! Come back!" He screamed. I felt bad but I wasn't gonna say anything to Rick.

We continued down the road when we got stuck in some mud near a bunch of abandoned cars. There were dead bodies and dismembered body parts lying around. Michonne pressed down on pedal, attracting walkers.

They banged on the windows and clawed at the for handles.

"Cover your ears." Rick ordered, slightly opening his window to sick his gun out.

bang

bang

bang

Soon all the walkers were dead and my ears were ringing.

We got out of the car to try and get it out of the mud. Michonne stayed in the dithers seat, while the rest of us looked for some cloth to create traction under the wheels.

"Yeah this'll work." Rick pulled a purple sheey out of a large suitcase in one of the cars.

"Tell me when." Michonne said from behind the steering wheel.

Carl was leaned against a car a few feet away, staring at the ground.

"Come watch. Learn something." I said, walking towards Rick. I heard Carl sigh and stomp over.

"Put something under the wheels like this with a little gravel and sticks. Gives hit traction." Rick said, sliding the sheet under the wheel with rocks underneath it.

"Wouldn't have to if she didn't get us in to this." Carl growled, according to Michonne.

"Hey." I scolded.

"It was a honest mistake. Could happen to anybody." Rick said firmly. I tapped the hood when Rick was done, signaling Michonne to start the car.

"Hey! Help me! Don't leave! Please!" The man from before had caught up and was yelling from a distance away.

"Rick..."

"No."

We got into the car and drove away from the dead bodies and screaming man.

A few minutes passed and we had entered Rick and Carls home town. It seemed like a nice place at first. We turned a few couriers and saw burned bodies, arrows pointing in the opposite direction and the streets covered in booby-traps.

Sharpened sticks, cages, metal spikes, and barbed wire lined the streets.

"What is all this?" Carl asked.

"I don't know."

--*

Forty-four

Did y'all notice the titles

I hate up in coming up for names for each so this happened

..yeah..

*_*_*

Alyx's POV

"Be careful, Carl." I warned as we walked along the side the traps and wires. His bright eyes slightly peered beneath his old hat, glaring harshly. I ignored him and took in the unique surroundings.

They were insane and terrifying, yet I admired the complexity. Each trap was very simple, but very effective.

I watched a lone walker, a young woman with a ripped up party dress, slowly get entangled in the traps. There was a small cage full of rodents surrounded by barbed wire and large wooden spikes. The walker took note of the live creature and stumbled towards it, embedding itself into the sharp edges and slicing through its skin.

Crimson blood poured into the ground, yet the living dead didn't seem to care.

"Alyx." Michonne harshly whispered, as she, Rick and Carl were yards ahead of me. I shook my head to try and focus on the actual task here.

Get in, get ammo, get out.

I jogged to keep up with them and walked by Michonne side. I trusted her, but not as much as I trust Rick.

"There's the police department a few ways down. If that place is cleared I know some smaller places we can go." I nodded subtly, and trudged along. This was going to be difficult, because of how easy it was so far.

We walked for a few more minutest not silence. Only the sound of walker groans and our heels clicking against the pavement.

Rick sighed heavily and pointed to a building a few yards in front of us.

"There it is. I'll go on first, Alyx you watch the back." We wandered in, carefully peering around each corner. Every few minutes, Rick would hold out his hand, telling us to stop. Each time was a surprise, causing me to bump into Carl. He would give me a dirty look each time.

We ran into a few walkers, taking them each down with ease.

Rough hangs grasped around my neck and pulled me back. I tried to scream for help, but one of the hands clasped around my mouth.

This wasn't a walker.

I used the heel of my boot to harshly kick one of his legs out from under the attacker. I assumed it was a man, given the tall and broad build.

As he was on the ground, I quickly gripped my machine gun and aimed it at the predator.

"Who are you?" I growled, kicking his shoulder aggressively. He slowly sat up with his hands raised.

"Please..." His voice was very deep and raspy, sounding as if he hasn't spoken in months. I tilted my head and squinted.

"Who are you?" I asked again, this time with much force. I heard a quiet growl coming from behind me and whipped around to kill the incoming walker. As I aimed and prepared to shoot, I was knocked to the ground and fell unconscious.

--*

"Daryl? Daryl!" I yelled into the empty house, kicking open the front door. "Daryl, get your ass down here and help me carry in this shit!"

"What?" He stumbled off the couch in some old boxers and a ripped up T-shirt. Scratching his chin, he pulled on some socks and helped carry in the rest of the groceries.

"Guess what I found?" I asked, excitingly.

"What'ya find?"

"You gotta guess. At least once." He groaned and sat on a stool near the kitchen table.

"A unicorn? Shotgun? Toilet paper? Dollhouse?" I shook my head after each answer.

"Nope, but good guesses." I started emptying the bags and putting the items away.

"So? What's the thing?" He asked, a little frustrated. I smirked and pulled it out from one of the paper bags. He gasped and his eyes went wide.

"Oh, Hell yeah!" He grabbed the almost brand new leather vest from my hands. It was one just like Merle's, only a little smaller and more detailed angle wings on the back. "Where'd ya find this?"

"Well, that's not really important. Try it on!" He gave me a suspicious look and threw the vest over his broad shoulders. It fit comfortably and made him look good.

"You're a doll." He ran up to me and picked me up in his arms.

"You don't gotta tell me." I gave a wide smile and he planted a sloppy kiss on my cheek.

--*

I was woken up by a soft kick at my side.

"Let's go." The same deep voice from before had been speaking above me. "Wake up!"

The man had dark skin, with eyes to match. Ragged clothes, knee pads, bulletproof vest, face mask. He was ready to fight.

I looked around. All kinds of guns littered the room I was a being held captive in. I attempted to jump at the man, but thick ropes tied my wrists to the pole of a small bed.

"I'll be back." He said and ran out of the room and down a flight of stairs. All across the walls were different sayings.

Everyone turns

I need to Clear

Higher ground

Duane turned

Many gunshots went off outside. I heard faint screaming and rustling from multiple people. I looked around the room, hoping to find something sharp to cut the rope.

All of my weapons were confiscated, including the small knife I hid in my boot.

I cursed under my breath, desperate for a knife of some sort. There was a small glass vase on the dresser beside me, which gave me an idea.

I lifted my boot up to my hands and untied the laces and pulled it off. My wrists were very restricted so it was hard to throw it at the vase, but I managed. It shattered on the ground, bits of broken glass everywhere.

The gunshots and the screaming from outside came to a halt

"Shit."

I hurriedly reached up foot to my hand again and pulled off my sock. My leg stretched off the bed, and like a monkey, I grabbed the biggest piece of glass I could reach.

"Finally." I muttered, exchanging the glass between my foot and hand. The rope was thick and the glass was dull, but after a few minutes, it cut through.

After I was cut free, I put my shoe back on and rubbed my sore wrist. The first thing I did once I was ready, was grab a sniper and look out the window.

Rick, Michonne and Carl were huddled near a shop across the street. I didn't want to scream or make any noise, so I waved as big as I could. Carl pointed in my direction, getting the attention of the other 2.

As they turned to look at me, I could now see what they were huddled around. It was my attacker. I gestured for them to come to the building I was in, and they nodded. Rick and Michonne picked up the man, and dragged him in my direction.

I was confused. This attacker just tried to kill all 3 of us, and now they were helping him. I raised my eyebrow at Carl and he waved it off.

Once I heard the coming up the stairs, I started looking around at all the weaponry.

"Rick? What the hell?" I said as I pointed at the man.

"I knew him. In the beginning, he saved my life." I have him a questioning glance, and he shrugged off.

"So? What are we gonna do?" I asked him, as his eyes wandered around the room. He was reading the walls, and his face dropped on "Duane turned".

"We're gonna wait for him to wake up."

Hours passed, and nothing was happening. I was on watch and every now and then, a walker would stumble by and get caught in the traps. It was quite amusing.

"Dad? You know that baby store a few blocks away?" Carl asked Rick. "The one moms friend Sarah owned?" Rick nodded subtly.

"Well I was thinking, now that Judith is getting bigger, she's gonna need a crib."

"Carl." Rick said, firmly.

"It's just around the corner! And there's all those walker traps." He persuaded. Rick quoted and tilted his head. He wasn't convinced.

"You're gonna need help carrying the box." Michonne pipped in.

"What?" Carl questioned.

"If you're gonna get a crib, you have to get a box. It's big and heavy. You're gonna need help carrying the box." She explained. "I'll go with him." She said to Rick.

"Alright, that's the deal. You need help, you holler. Me and Alyx will come running." Michonne nodded and Carl frowned.

They left shortly, Rick and I sat in silence. There's was some rustling coming from the man, who I learned was called Morgan. We watched him like a hawk as he turned on his side in his sleep.

Suddenly he jumped up, knife in his hand, crazy look on his face. He slashed at me, leaving a long cut across my collarbone. I gasped and fell back, trying to stop the bleeding.

He then attacked Rick, tackling him to the ground in a few seconds. He kicked Morgan off, pulling out his gun and aiming it at his head.

"Do you know who I am? Do you see who I am?" Rick asked.

"Dead people wearing dead people's faces!" He yelled.

"Morgan, listen to me." Rick said, slowly lowering his gun, trying too reason with the man.

"No, I don't know you!"

"You do know me."

"I don't know you."

"You saved my life, Morgan."

"I don't know you!" Morgan screamed and ran up, tackling Rick to the ground. Morgan yanked his knife out again and plunged it into Ricks shoulder. I tried to get up and help, but the amount of bleeding was making me light headed, I didn't get that far.

"Look at me!" Rick yelled and pushed Morgan off of him. He stood up and pointed his gun and Morgan once more.

"You don't clear, man. You turn. You just die!" He was crying and screaming. His hands balled into right fists as he sat back on his heels. He was clearly done fighting.

"You know me!" Rick said again.

"I don't know anyone anymore. You don't clear anymore."

"You know me." Rick said it quieter this time, more force and anger. "You crazy son of a bitch." He rose his gun and lined it up with Morgan's forehead. I wasn't sure if he was going to shoot or not.

"Please...Please kill me. Just kill me, Just kill me." Morgan grabbed Ricks gun and held it again this head. Rick rolled it out of his grip and tucked it away.

"You found me last year in my front lawn, Morgan. You and... you found me. You fed me, you told me what happened. You saved me. My name is Rick Grimes. You know me. I'm not wearing a dead man's face." He picked up a walkie-talkie that was in a bin nearby. "I gave you this. I said I'd turn it on every day at dawn so you could find me."

"Rick? I know you. Damn it, I ... I know you. I know who you are. You said you'd turn yours on at dawn. That's what you said. I mean, I hadn't worked up to it yet, and ... then I did. On the roof, every morning for days, for weeks, me and my boy. And then... me. Just static, though. Nothing but static. And then nothing but nothing. You weren't there. You were never there."

"I was." Rick said.

" Not when I tried. I mean, you said you would turn on your radio every day at dawn."

"Morgan... I-"

"You said that you would!"

"I did."

"...Everyday at dawn. You were never there!"

Rick was running his hands through his hair and pacing around the room, obviously frustrated. I was beyond confused, learning so much about Ricks past in such a short amount of time.

"kept getting ... I kept getting pushed farther out. I had to. I didn't have a choice. I found my wife and my boy. I had people. I had to keep them safe. We kept getting pushed back deeper into the country. I swear to God I didn't have a choice."

"You can have your radio back. Looks like I finally found you. You found your wife and your son. That's what happened, right? You found them. Did they ... Did she ... did your wife ... did she turn?" Morgan asked, still sitting on the floor, too tired to move.

"No, she died. "

"So you didn't have to see that, then."

"Of course not. "

"Not like me. "

"No."

"Not like me. Not like my wife. You remember what happened to her? You remember what she was?"

"Yeah."

"Oh. You gave me the gun. You tried."

"What did I try, Morgan? What did I try?"

"You tried to get me to do it 'cause I was supposed to do it. I was supposed to kill her, my Jenny. Knew I was supposed to, but I let it go. Let it go like there wasn't gonna be a reckoning. We was always looking for food. You know, it always came down to food. And I was ... I was checking out a cellar and I didn't want Duane to come down there with me. And then when I came up... she was standing there right in front of him and he had his gun up and he couldn't do it. So I called to him and he turned. And then she was just ... on him. And I see red. I see red. Everything is red. Everything I see is red. And I do it. Finally. Finally was too late. I was supposed to. I was selfish. I was weak. You gave me the gun... Hey, your boy ... is he dead?"

"No."

"No? He will be. See, 'cause people like you, the good people, they always die, And the bad people do, too. But the weak people, the people like me... we have inherited the Earth."

--*

a lot of dialogue towards the end because I didn't know how to really write that scene, ya know? anyway this may be one of the longest chapters I have written. I know, pathetic.

aight

also I didn't edit it so mistakes left and right whoops

Forty-five

70 THOUSANDS READS??????? SPANK ME WITH RAW TUNA AND SHIT IN THE SAVANNAH

THATS OUTRAGEOUS

i def dont deserve that but thx ily

Also my computer keeps changing Michonne to Machine

*_*_*

Alyx's POV

After a lengthy attempt to get Morgan to come join us at the prison, Rick finally let it go. They bickered for almost an hour before Rick caved in. Morgan reused to come back with us, claiming it would be gone in days. Carl and Michonne returned shortly after the argument with a pink and brown crib, a photograph and colorful cat statue. Michonne said she couldn't leave the statue behind, because of its beauty, which caused me to laugh for the first time in a while. I don't know much about the photograph except that it was of the Grimes family from years ago and that Carl went through hell to get it.

As the 4 of us were leaving Morgans town, his actions caught our attention. He was searching through his traps, killing any walkers who fell for them and laying them neatly on a gurney. From the piles of burnt bodies around town, I figured thats how he disposes of them.

"He's okay?" Michonne asked, surprised to see him walking around after they knocked him out beforehand. Rick shook his head and walked a few feet ahead of us.

"No, he's not." He said with a rough tone and a frown on his face.

"Wait." Carl stopped us and let down his end of the crib we were carrying. "Hey!" He called out to Morgan. Rick put his hand on his sons shoulder to shush him, but Carl ignored his father. "Morgan!" Carl called again."I had to shoot you. You know I had to, right?"

Morgan nodded firmly, a frown permanetly etched onto his face.

"I'm sorry." Carl apologized. He started to walk again, but Morgan stomped towards Carl. I thought he was going to hurt him, so I discreetly pulled out my knife and held it behind my back.

"Hey, son." Morgan said. "Don't ever be sorry." Carl nodded. I put away my knife, and we rushed away from the town full of traps.

*_*_*

Michonne and I were a few steps behind Carl and Rick once we left the small town. They seemed to be having some sort of discussion about Michonne, since they turned and glanced at her a few times. She seemed curious, as was I, but Rick smiled at the end of their conversation so it was probably positive.

"I think they want you to stay." I said to Michonne beside me. She shook her head.

"No." She said simply, and grumpily.

"I've known them for a while now. It seems like they do." I glanced beside me at the intimidating woman to find her staring straight ahead.

"No." She repeated firmly. I shrugged it off, but I could tell Rick, Carl and I saw something in her.

All 4 of us placed the guns and other supplies we gathered into the trunk of the car. Carl and I unloaded our supplies quicker than Rick and Michonne, causing a small split in our group.

"What do you think of her?" I asked Carl quietly. A ghost of a smile appeared on his lips as he answered.

"I think she's one of us." I grinned and ran my fingers through my mop of dark hair.

"Me too, Carl. Me too."

The ride home was silent. Silent and awkward. Especially awkward after we stopped next to the fresh carcass of the man we ignored beforehand, just to steal his backpack full of supplies. A bright orange knapsack drizzled with fresh blood and rotted skin. While the outside was repulsive, the contents were the opposite. 2 cans of beans, 4 boxes of ammo, 3 bottles water and a few peices of spare clothing filled it to the brim. I smiled, then grimaced when I released how twisted that act was. To find joy in the death of a stranger. An innocent stranger. I sighed and stared out my dirty passenger window.

The situation the world enduring was terrifying and gruesome, yet the environment was radiant. The forests trees covered in bright green algae and bold flowers scattered across the dirt covered ground. The suns rays shined between the dark branches, lighting up every detail in its surroundings. Wild animals skipping by without a care in the world.

We turned a few corners and the beauty I was gratefully observing was gone in a heartbeat. Instead of algae covering the plants, it was dried blood. Instead of flowers littering the ground, it was rotting bodies. No more animals skipping by; only the undead.

Moments passed and we finally arrived at the Prison. Carol greeting us happily at the gate, while we had the opposite feelings. Rick, Carl, Michonne and I were highly devastated from our previous discoveries. I flicked Carl's hat and patted Ricks shoulder as we walked into the prison together.

I immediately dropped off my gatherings in the common room and trudged to my cell, where I flopped onto the small bed. As I laid on the shitty and small comforter, I got an idea. I had some free time, some motivation and a need for a double bed. Might as well surprise Daryl too. I hopped out of bed and down the stairs, stopping right in front of Merles cell.

"Whadda want from me, girlie?" His raspy voice asked me without even glancing in my direction. I sighed and slowly blinked.

"I need your help."

"You? Need MY help?" He laughed. "Help fromme!" He laughed again.

"Shut the fuck up and come help me fuck something up."

"Now that... I can do!"

I quickly told him about my simple plan to make our cell 40 times more enjoyable. Both Daryl and I understand the shitty world we live in and I figured a splash of something nice would be good for the both of us.

As we moved around me and Daryl's few belongings, we were mostly quiet.

"Where is Daryl, anyway?" I asked. Merle smirked and shrugged.

"Honestly not sure. My baby bro loves to wonder off, ya know tha'." I nodded and chuckled sarcastically.

"I sure do." Merle began searching each empty cell for another bed without a top bunk, and after a few minutes we managed to find one. He pushed it into my room and against the bed already in here. It looked like crap, but slightly nicer crap than before.

"I'll be back." I said before rushing off to find any sort of storage closet nearby. Finally finding a small one, I searched through it before finding fresh sheets and a thick quilt-like blanket. I gathered as much as my arms would let me and brought them to my cell, laying them nicely on the double bed.

"Sweet." I said and flopped down once again, this time a noticeable difference in comfort. "Really sweet." I heard Merle chuckle from behind me and I grimaced.

"Get out Merle." His chuckle faded and he slapped his knee before exiting and returning to where he belongs.

A laid for minutes before I kicked off my shoes and climbed under the fresh covers, falling asleep with no problem at all.

*_*_*

this was trash and I hope for death

fourty-six. the end

15 years later

"But what ever happened with the governor? Did you and daddy beat him? Was Michonne allowed in the group? You have to tell me the rest!" She said.

"Harley! Enough questions, baby. I'll finish the story when your older. But for now, she did join our group and we did beat him." I answered my daughter. Every night for the past year I've explained how Daryl and I survived the 'end of the world'. Only, it wasn't the end. We beat our enemies, found new people, a new home, and survived until a cure was found.

A cure and vaccine was created in 2019, 10 years ago. There was an international broadcasting from the French, explaining to the remaining population how we would all need create our own versions of the medicine.